T0024743

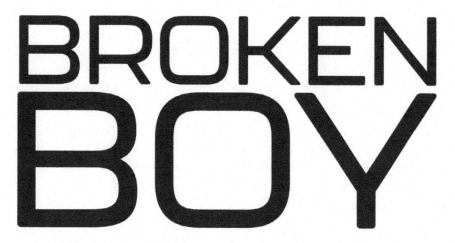

BROKEN BOY

Surviving Foster Care and Giving Back to the System That Stole My Childhood

G.V. MEDEIROS

BROKEN BOY

Surviving Foster Care and Giving Back to the System That Stole My Childhood

Copyright © 2024 by Gino V. Medeiros

Printed in the United States of America

Website: *www.ginomedeiros.com*

BookBaby Publishing
www.bookbaby.com

ISBN: 979-8-35094-284-2

For Juju

Who knew when to hold me tightly
and when to let me go
who made room in her heart
for everything I brought with me
and everything I would become
who taught me how to be the man I am
and how to carry on her legacy
of unconditional faith,
unwavering kindness,
and uncompromising compassion.

Thank you for being exactly the mother I
needed at exactly the right time.

CONTENTS

Family dysfunction rolls down from generation to generation, like a fire in the woods, taking down everything in its path until one person in one generation has the courage to turn and face the flames. That person brings peace to their ancestors and spares the children that follow.

TERRY REAL

Do the best you can until you know better. Then, when you know better, do better.

MAYA ANGELOU

Prologue

It's adoption day. I am sitting perched on a stool at the breakfast bar in the kitchen fiddling with the computer and waiting for a selection of family and friends to come online. And the judge, of course. I keep telling myself this hearing is just a legal formality. It doesn't really matter. There's no reason to be as nervous and giddy as a little kid, but my hands are shaking. I'm not a kid. I'm fifty years old.

Juju sits next to me. Her shrinking frame swims in a T-shirt emblazoned with the slogan "Out of my way, it's finally adoption day!" The shirts were my idea, but she insisted on the after-party replete with a sprinkle-covered cake with "It's a boy!" written across it in blue icing. As I set up the computer, she chatters incessantly at my husband, Tony. She's always been chatty, but now even more so. She uses what she calls "interviewing" others to try to make her memory loss less noticeable.

Today she will officially become my mother in the eyes of the state. I've thought of her as my mom for the last thirty-four years, even though I call her Juju. The name came from my niece, who, as a toddler, couldn't pronounce "Judy." It stuck, and we've been calling her Juju ever since.

People have always commented on how much we look and act alike despite not being biologically related. Like me, Juju is blue-eyed and, before age silvered her locks and thinned mine, we both sported golden, flax-fine hair (although she was always the first to point out hers was from a bottle).

Despite her physical health problems and early signs of Alzheimer's, she still sparkles with exuberance, humor, and kindness above all.

We've spent the morning bustling around together making final arrangements for the intimate gathering that will follow the online hearing. The paperwork was submitted and approved months ago, so today is really just for the family. I am blessed with a happy marriage, have adopted two teenage kids of my own, have two amazing stepchildren, a wide extended support network, and have fought through the challenges of my early years with therapy, pets, books, and love. Juju is my mom. Everyone knows it. This hearing is just the next logical step. It doesn't really matter, I remind myself.

Just the same, when Tony comes up behind me and puts a warm hand on my shoulder, I feel calmer and let go of some of the tension I was holding. He doesn't say anything. He doesn't need to. He always knows how I'm feeling, often before I do. He is my rock, solid, strong, and gentle. At six feet tall, I tower over him, but he matches my active, occasionally manic energy (another trait I share with Juju) with gentle simplicity and quiet kindness. He doesn't say much, but when he does, his words are thoughtfully chosen. His fierce intelligence is matched only by his humility.

It's two o'clock. My family and some longtime friends are now all online and the judge, a kindly older gentleman with an amused smile, appears in the upper left of my screen.

"Good afternoon, everyone," the judge says. He was surprised when he received the request. Adult adoptions are rare. However, in reading the story of my childhood and my relationship with Juju and witnessing her vivacity, he was tickled to be a part of this belated ritual.

It was while caring for Juju after her second stroke that she brought up the idea of adoption. By this point, her mental state was in deep decline, but she was as clever and sociable as ever. She had even managed to convince one of her doctors she had been part of a secret anti-terrorist task force and a CIA operative. The doctor had come out of her hospital room and thanked me for her service. I clued him in. Almost nothing Juju had told him was true, no matter how charming and matter-of-fact she was in her delivery. He was shocked and responded by telling me what I already knew—Juju should no longer live alone.

It just made sense for Juju to stay with me and Tony rather than my having to manage her care from the other end of the San Francisco Bay Area.

One day, as we were driving in the car somewhere, she piped up from the back seat, "I wonder why I never adopted you."

"It's not too late," I said. "We still can if you want to."

"It would make it easier, in terms of caregiving, if you were officially family in the eyes of the state," said Tony.

"What do you think?" I asked Juju, glad she brought it up in a moment of mental clarity.

"Yes," she said. "Yes, I'd like that."

Now here we are, huddled around the breakfast bar. The judge peers through his glasses and signs the papers with a flourish.

"I have now affixed my signature to it. It is now official. Congratulations, Mom. Congratulations, Son."

Tony's hand tightens on my shoulder as tears stream down my face. Even though it's just the proclamation of a stranger on a computer screen, the judge recognizing us as family in front of our loved ones fills a hole in me I had almost forgotten was there. I am surrounded by people who care about me in a home I helped build. It's a normal life with all its ups and downs, squabbles, laughter, drama, and love.

It does matter. It has always mattered. Kindness matters. Family matters. Closure matters. Forgiveness matters. Most of all, belonging matters.

It's important you know this is how the story ends. No matter how difficult it gets, life is a gift. To get to the good part, I had to face the bad part head-on. There were many I grew up with who were less fortunate, who became statistics, victims of an unwanted childhood. I faced my demons with the compassion and kindness of my family. Now it is my turn to shed a light on the system I was raised in with all its problems and potential, share just how vital the gift of belonging is and how we, as a society, can do a better job of making sure no child grows up alone.

CHAPTER 1

Background of Trauma

Jaquelin Joan Davis, known to everyone as Jackie, was a beautiful woman. She had a slender frame, sweet face with large, gentle eyes, and flowing ebony locks. As with many survivors of sexual abuse, her looks were both her burden and her shield. Her features kept people at a distance, her body and face were decoys she could sacrifice to prevent anyone from getting too close to her heart. It was a strategy I myself became all too familiar with as a young man.

She met Gene Binsbachar, Sr. in 1968 when he was on leave from the hospital in Santa Rosa, California, about an hour north of San Francisco. It was a warm night known as "Cruising Night" where everyone drove their cars up and down the main street. He was a handsome man in a crisp uniform with big dreams of success. Having been sent home from Vietnam with a leg wound, he was allowed to leave the hospital on weekends. When he met Jackie, he was smitten. She was seventeen years old, and he was twenty— exactly the right ages to mistake lust for true love. They were married only a few months later. When his leg had healed and he was ordered to Camp Pendleton in Southern California, she went with him. They lived there for a time until he was released from active duty. In a letter he wrote me much later, he described that period as "the best we had."

When he was released from the military, they moved back to Santa Rosa and in with his mother, Florence, whom we all called "Nonni." Gene got a job in a lumber yard to pay the bills. It didn't take him long to figure out that manual labor was not the path to a successful future. He started attending night school to get his college degree. Unfortunately, this meant Jackie was left alone most of the time. She started finding companionship in the arms of other men barely a year after their wedding.

When Gene moved from the lumber yard to a more lucrative and responsible job with the Greyhound bus company, both his absences and her cheating got worse. The couple broke up and got back together time and again until one huge fight where she said she would leave him for the last time. What she didn't know was that she was already pregnant with his child. When she found out, they decided to give it another try. She was barely nineteen at the time.

Nonni insisted on naming the newborn son after his father: Gene Weldon Binsbachar, Jr. Jackie wanted him to be named after Nonni's father, Gino. Ultimately, a compromise was reached. I was named Gene but raised as Gino. In later life, having no ties to my father and seeing no reason to keep his name, I had it legally changed to Gino.

Six months after I was born, Gene caught Jackie cheating again. They were divorced soon after, and Gene left to start a new life elsewhere. He sent regular child support payments, but Jackie was never good with money and seemed perpetually balanced on the very edge of poverty.

I was very close to my mother during those early years. Since my father wasn't in the picture much, she was all I had. She adored me, and when things were good, they were great. She married again when I was one or two. My new stepfather came from a wealthy ranching family and owned a clothing store. He treated us very well.

My mother loved to take me shopping with her newfound wealth. She showered me with toys and darted around clothing stores finding outfits for me to wear. My shoes were always white despite my little-boy knack of getting them dirty almost immediately.

On my second birthday, however, she went above and beyond. I raced out of my room to see what new goodies awaited me to find Jackie, her husband, Johnny, and her mother, Lucille, waiting for me in the living room. Jackie beamed at me and led me outside. Confused, I lagged behind.

"Come on, little Lord Fauntleroy!" said Grandma Lucille. This was her term of endearment for me in my ever-changing and extravagant wardrobe. "Your present's out here."

I ran outside into the cool morning air to see what it was. There stood a full-size quarter horse.

"Her name's Coco," said Jackie. I was a bit taken aback, but she hoisted me up to sit astride the horse. I still have a picture of me sitting on Coco looking confused. The extraordinary and inappropriate gift for a two-year-old was Jackie to a T. All I yearned for was her time and affection. Instead, I got gifts.

Often, I was left in the care of my grandma Lucille. She was a feisty lady and I kept her on her toes by getting into trouble, but she adored me. In addition to "little Lord Fauntleroy," she sometimes called me "Binky" because I had been obsessed with my binky as a baby. Her house featured a large planter she kept at the bottom of the stairs. It was of a kind that was popular in the '70s, with a large glass globe on top of a slender concrete plinth. One of the many times she was watching me, I had done something to make her angry and she was chasing me through the house with a wooden spoon. I was a good runner even then. The harder she tried to catch me, the madder she got and the funnier I thought it was. I was screeching with laughter and tearing through the house on my stubby little legs, when I rounded the bottom of the stairs at an unstable gallop, crashed into the planter, and down it went. The crash resounded throughout the house. My eyes got as big as dinner plates. I was in big trouble now! But by the time she caught me, Grandma Lucille just scooped me up and burst into laughter.

"Oh, Binky. What am I chasing you for? It's not even worth it!" She laughed with me, hugging me tightly and kissing my forehead with tears running down her face.

I don't know why Jackie's second marriage failed, but when it did, the money dried up almost overnight. It was around this time my memories of my childhood became much clearer. Often, those who suffer and struggle as children repress traumatic memories, but mine have always remained clear, vivid, and ever present. Throughout the difficult times that followed, I found comfort in the reminders that I was still alive. No matter how bad things got, I would persevere.

When Jackie's second marriage ended, one of the things we kept was a sleek black sports car I later learned was a Pontiac GTO. It was one of the few things we owned. I have a vivid memory of it being stolen, adding another blow to our financial troubles. It was found on the side of the freeway stripped and sitting on blocks. I still remember Jackie swearing and screaming at the police when we were shown the car—the last vestige of the good life now a skeleton in a ditch.

The next car she could afford was far less glamorous. It was an old coupe with a hard top I later identified as a Ford Thunderbird. It soon became not only our car, but our home. To me at that age, living in the car was an adventure. It had a passenger door that wouldn't latch completely and would fly open as we went around corners. After a few terrifying drives, she figured out a way to tie it shut, but the despair I felt weighing on her heart is tangible to me even now.

After living in the car for a while, we were able to move into a small, pink, one-bedroom cottage in a row of identical attached cottages. My mother had a male "friend" named Wayne who was always around. Wayne drove a gigantic Cadillac. Whenever he came to visit, I was told to go outside and wait on the porch. I would hear my mother making loud noises inside and I was sure he was beating her up. I hated Wayne, but I had figured out men were often the reason we had a place to live. He wasn't beating her up, of course. I didn't learn about sex until later, and then all too soon.

I was very effeminate as a young child. At first, I suspect, she thought it was cute, but as I got older, she became concerned. Jackie was raised in an environment that did not tolerate nonconforming boys. She was the first in a long line of caregivers who had no idea how to handle my affections. When I was three or four, she asked me what I wanted for my birthday. When I announced I wanted a pretty dress, she was stunned.

This is when she started leaving me alone with her male partners and friends. In her defense, I'm sure she felt leaving me with men would teach me to be more "masculine." What she didn't realize was that I was trying to be like her. I missed her and just wanted to be closer to her. I am certain my mother felt leaving me with those men was best for me. I have never faulted her for doing so. But this sort of desperate neglect was the beginning of a pattern that changed the course of my childhood. Some of the men had sex with girlfriends while I was there. Some got drunk or did drugs. One or two touched me. One beat up our dog. I don't remember any of their names or faces, but I still remember the sound of that little beagle crying.

None of them, of course, did anything to provide the care a child needs. Even though much of the abuse I suffered later while in the foster care system was perpetrated by women, I still held a deep-seated mistrust of men—a scar left over from this time in my life.

The worst of these men was my grandfather Jack, my mother's father. The things he did to me devastated my soul. My mother left me with him and his second wife, Zola, many times when I was a little boy. (Lucille had divorced him before I was born.) Just as he had abused my mother, her sister, and her brother, he began abusing me. It wasn't until I was in my twenties that Jackie told me he had done the same to her. Then, in my thirties, I heard a similar story from her sister.

The memory of being molested at this age has been with me my entire life, but it was not until I was in my mid-teens that I realized that the person who had done the molesting was my own grandfather. I had always assumed it was a foster parent, which, in a way, may have been easier to cope with. The notion that my own grandfather could do those things to me was very difficult to come to terms with.

He was good at seducing me; I am almost ashamed to admit. In a twisted way, I may have looked forward to it. I was starved for attention. In addition to being effeminate, I was also sensitive and desperate to make sure everyone around me was happy. Empathy and the desire to please is a child molester's way in. My grandfather used my own body against me. He started by paying a little too much attention to my "private area" when he'd give me a bath, and he *always* gave me my bath when I stayed with him. He would masturbate me with his hand and "talk me through" the process. Although I had no way of knowing what was going on at that age, I knew it felt good, and it seemed to make my grandfather very happy. Every time we finished my bath he would say, "Wasn't that fun, Gino? Didn't Grandpa make you feel good?"

Courtesy of my grandfather and his hand, I discovered, at the age of three or four, the intense feeling of an orgasm. My mother often found me sleeping with my pants down around my ankles, thumb in my mouth, and sound asleep. He had taught me how to masturbate before I went to sleep. He told me it would relax me and make it easier to sleep. But my little body didn't know how to process the intense physical sensation that an orgasm brings. I would fall dead asleep in an instant with my pants still around my ankles when I was done. How my mother didn't catch on is beyond me. Denial is a powerful force.

Over time, Jack graduated from hand jobs in the bathtub to performing oral sex on me while I slept. He used to say he loved to watch me wake up with a smile on my face. I can't say it hurt, and even though I sensed it was wrong somehow, the idea of keeping a secret made me feel special and in control. I can't even say I felt dirty during or immediately after Jack did his thing; that didn't come until later in life. The attention Jack gave me was so welcome that I began to try to figure out ways to be alone with him. Jack's location of choice for our "play time" was his house when no one else was home, but I can also recall several trips to the store in Grandpa's truck that involved my head in his lap.

Eventually Jack graduated to inviting me into *his* bed. If someone were to ask me today to describe Jack in detail, I would be hard-pressed to do so. I have memories of some of his more prominent features. I remember he was a large man with a big stomach. When Jack invited me to his bed, it was done in a way that made me feel special, important, and loved. The process was almost a ritual—a rite of passage. He would strip naked and, I believe purposefully, make me undress myself as he lay and watched. I suppose this was his way of making what we were doing seem voluntary. When I was naked, he would hoist me up and lay me on top of his bulbous stomach. I was a small child, so when I was lying on his stomach, my arms and my feet didn't reach the bed; they sort of dangled and hung off the side of his belly. I can almost smell him as I write this. Even with his mouth closed he smelled of tobacco and whisky. He had a tracheotomy hole in his throat, and I could smell his breath through the hole. Despite the hole and the smell of his breath, I remember I adored him. He always made me feel like I was the most important person in the world.

Jack's final act of seduction was what he called "his turn." He would say something like, "Don't you want to make Grandpa feel as good as he makes you feel when you wake up from your naps?" Of course I did! I loved him! He was my grandpa! Jack taught me how to perform oral sex on him when I was around three years old.

Of all the things he said to me during my time with him, this stands out the most: "You are such a beautiful boy, Gino! Do you know how beautiful you are, my sweet boy?" Now just writing those words sends a wave of nausea through me.

To this day I am uncomfortable when I look at pictures of myself as a little boy. There is a little part of me that wonders—still—if it was me that seduced him. I know, in my conscious, logical, adult mind, that's ridiculous. I was an innocent victim, a child. But I was my mother's son, an attractive—almost pretty—boy. Maybe I learned to use that in my favor? So goes the monologue of self-blame in my mind that has played over and over my whole life. When I see pictures of myself as a little boy, I wonder what I was thinking and if I somehow invited it. I suppose this is what a child predator does best: use a child's own body and mind as a weapon.

As I got older, I came to believe masturbation and the resulting orgasm were bad and dirty things. I treated my own body with complete disregard as a young adult. How I managed to navigate my twenties without contracting any life-threatening diseases will always be a mystery to me. No one can be that lucky. Perhaps Lucille was watching over me. As I have gotten older, with the exception of Jack's version of "special time," memories of him have faded. Many years later, when I was reunited with my birth mother and shown pictures of him, the sight of him made me feel sick. I never told her that.

By the time I was five, I was already a seasoned latchkey kid. My mother was working as a bartender, and her life revolved around honky-tonk bars and the men they catered to. She wasn't around much but managed to round up another string of questionable babysitters for me. I often ended up being the one doing the babysitting while they ranted, pontificated, or slept through whatever they were on. I learned the smell of marijuana very early. She did the best she could with what she had, but there were obvious problems that the world at large was beginning to notice. I was sent to kindergarten unwashed and in dirty clothes, often with no lunch. I don't remember much about the escalation that led to me being removed from her care. It gets lost in the string of people that rotated through our lives, but I sense teachers became concerned, or perhaps a relative, which led to Child Protective Services getting involved.

I didn't learn this until much later, but at this time, there were several family members, including Grandma Lucille, who offered to take me in. They could see Jackie wasn't coping as a mother, and the writing was on the wall that I would be remanded to the custody of the state. One of these people may even have reported the situation to CPS. Unfortunately for me, all these offers came with a caveat: Jackie would have no say in how I was raised. There would be no back-and-forth. Even though she couldn't handle taking care of me herself, she refused time and again to let me go. This selfishness is something that took a long time for me to forgive and created a deep rift between Jackie and some members of her family. Sometimes, I must remind myself she was only in her early twenties at the time and had very little that was truly hers, but it is difficult to know that I could have had a childhood in a loving home almost from the very beginning.

Despite this and everything that followed, I must acknowledge that for all its flaws, the foster care system did provide something my birth mother could never have given me—a fighting chance. It was a slim chance, just a small ray of hope, but in the end it was enough. There is not a single doubt in my mind—had I stayed and been raised by Jackie—I would have ended up on drugs, homeless, in jail, or dead in the gutter rather than in the loving home I now enjoy.

It's also important to note that this is how it always is. The children who enter the foster care system have already faced at least two layers of trauma: the abuse or neglect that caused them to be removed from their biological parents in the first place, and the trauma of the removal itself. For me, it was just a matter of time.

CHAPTER 2

The Institutional Solution

I was five years old and playing at a friend's house after school when the police came for me. We were lining up green plastic army men on the carpet in his living room when I heard a noise outside and went to the window. A black and white cruiser pulled up. Two uniformed officers got out and strode toward the front door.

"What's going on?" asked my friend, but I barely heard him. I was already in a state of panic. They were here for me. They were going to take me away. It's every child's worst nightmare and, somehow, I knew. The officers walked up to the porch and rang the bell. My friend's mom called, "Just a minute!" from the kitchen. I could feel cold sweat on my palms and hear her steps approaching to open the door. I couldn't stand it anymore. I raced out of the room and down the hall. I heard the door open and one of the officers say my name before I hurled myself to the floor in my friend's bedroom and squirmed under the bed.

It was in the corner of his room, so I scrunched myself as far up against the wall as I could and cried quietly. I could hear the officers and my friend's mom search through the house, feet clomping and items being shifted around as they called my name. She asked her son about me. "I don't know," he said. "He just ran off."

It took a long time, and some small part of me hoped they would give up and go away so I could go back home. I held my breath. The sounds grew nearer. I could tell the search had narrowed and the list of hiding places was getting short.

Finally, from my vantage under the bed, I saw a pair of shiny black shoes and the bottoms of blue trousers walk up. The officer got down on the floor and peered into my hiding place. He had been looking under every bed in the house.

"Hi there, Gino. Would you please come out? We'd like to talk with you." His manner was friendlier than I had expected, but it was clear I had no choice. I wiggled out onto the floor.

The police officers took me into the living room and sat me down on the couch. When they spoke, their tone was calm and polite, but I still didn't trust them. I asked what I had done wrong. They told me I wasn't in trouble, but just because I was five didn't mean I was stupid. The police don't come unless you're bad. It took them a while to convince me, but eventually, they were able to get me to start talking.

"Where is your mother now, Gino?"

"At the bar."

"Can you tell me about the bar? Do you know where it is?"

"Sure. I go there all the time. It's called Marty's. It's at the top of the hill."

At this, the officers and my friend's mom started looking uncomfortable, so I thought I'd offer something else.

"Do you want me to take you there?"

"That's okay. We know where it is."

At this point, I felt a little more confident. "Why are you here if you're not going to take me to jail?" I asked.

"Well," said one of the officers, exchanging a glance with the other, "there are a lot of people that are pretty worried about you."

Then he dropped the bombshell. "We'd like you to come with us some-where where you'll be safer."

"Uh…go where?"

"Just somewhere safe where you can be looked after for a while."

"Okay, but do I get to see my mommy so I can tell her I won't be home?"

They promised me I would.

I didn't see Jackie again for two years.

The place they took me was called the Dependent Unit. In 1975, this facility was housed in the old VA hospital in Santa Rosa, California. It was essentially a way station to house kids temporarily in an emergency situation once they became dependents of the court. Of course, if a placement failed, or if there was nowhere else to put them, some could expect much longer stays.

The police car pulled up the swooping drive to stop before a huge, Spanish-style building painted bright pink. I later learned the staffers had given it the ironic name the "Pink Palace." As we rolled to a stop, I peered out the reinforced window to see a woman come down the steps to meet us. She wore a white outfit similar to that of a nurse, down to the little hat, plus a chain of pink sparkling stones that hung from her horn-rimmed glasses. What she wasn't wearing was a smile. I thought it was odd that someone who matched the cheerful color scheme of the building so well should be so dour.

The police officers walked with me to the entrance, one on either side, each holding one of my hands. They took their time handing me off to the serious lady. As they did so, one of the officers bent down to my level. "Be strong, kiddo," he said. "You're going to be okay. Don't worry about your mommy. She knows where you are, and that you're safe." I never saw either of the officers again, but looking back at that moment, I realize it must have been a heartbreaking job to take children away from their parents.

The serious lady had no such compunctions. I felt like she was going to tear my arm out of the socket as she dragged me through the sterile hallways on the ground floor of the Pink Palace. After a long hall and a few turns, we arrived at a tiny intake office. It was furnished with an institutional metal desk with a fake wood-grain top, upon which sat a large manual typewriter. A single fluorescent light with gold louvres of the type popular at the time flickered overhead. It smelled like old lunch. The dour lady pulled out a clipboard with a thick stack of forms and started asking me questions. I was relieved to discover I knew all the answers. I rattled off my name, date of birth, address, and so forth. The lady never smiled, but at least seemed satisfied.

She picked up the phone on her desk, stabbed at the buttons with a stubby finger, and spoke in a bored monotone.

"Okay, we got a little guy here. Come get 'im."

She hung up and went back to the papers on her desk, without giving me another glance. I squirmed on my brown metal folding chair like a mouse in a trap waiting for an unknown fate. The only sound was the rattle of her pink glasses chain and the scratch of her pen as she filled out forms. My little feet dangled heavily, and my legs felt dead. When the door swung open, a gigantic Black man appeared in front of me. I felt my heart stop and my jaw drop. The man squeezed through the doorway. He might as well have been twelve feet tall.

He leaned down and spoke in a resonant baritone with a hint of country twang, "And what do we have here?"

I started to tremble in spite of myself. Through being taken by the police and all the questions from the serious lady, I had tried so hard to be strong, but I just couldn't hold it back anymore. I broke down in ragged sobs.

"WHOOA, little feller! There ain't nuthin' to be crying 'bout now." The giant got down on one knee and smiled with a kindness that filled his whole being. "You and me's gonna be pals! The name's Earl. Nice ta meechya."

By now Earl was down on his hands and knees, twisting his gigantic body so he could get his face down under mine, but there was no consoling me.

"Where's my mommy!?! I want my mommy!"

It was a question he must have heard a thousand times from a thousand frightened children. He looked up at the serious lady and sighed before twisting himself back down to talk to me from a nonthreatening position. "I knows, little guy. I knows."

I was scared, tired, and hungry, but Earl sat there twisted up beneath me and just patted my knee with one massive hand. He waited with gentle patience as I had my meltdown. The serious lady never looked up from her paperwork. When I had cried myself out, Earl said it wouldn't be much longer. Then I could rest.

He could have crushed my tiny hand with one squeeze, but as we walked down one of the identical white hallways tinged with the scent of industrial cleaner, he held on with a softness and kindness that quelled my tears and put me at ease. I later learned Earl was referred to as the "Gentle Giant" by everyone in the Pink Palace.

As we were walking down the hall, Earl explained to me what was going to happen next. I hung on to every word as he told me my hair would be cut short—buzzed to the scalp—and then I would have to take a very hot shower. He said the soap I had to use smelled yucky, but it was very important that I "wash real good wit it." I now know I was being deloused. Earl promised he would be right outside when I was finished.

At the end of my shower, Earl's gigantic arm came through the curtain with a towel. He told me there were clean pajamas on the chair in the bathroom and told me to come out when I had brushed my teeth. I did what I was told and, feeling somewhat better, rejoined Earl in the hall, where he took my hand again. I asked Earl where my clothes were. He told me I would get them back when I left. He explained all the kids in the Pink Palace shared clothes, and no one was allowed to have personal items. Personal items were stored and returned when you were "processed out."

Earl took me up what seemed like a mountain of stairs to another hall. Just around the corner from the stairwell was a huge double door. As we were just about to go through the doors, Earl told me this was where I'd be sleeping while I was there. He pushed open the swinging door, revealing a room full of steel-framed twin beds, fifteen or twenty of them. The bedding was the same on each: gray wool army blankets with white sheets. The thin mattresses sat on a series of intertwined springs. There were no other children in the room, but there was a massive Easter basket bursting with candy and toys sitting on one of the beds.

"That'd be your bed there, little guy." Earl pointed at the bed with the Easter basket on it. He didn't need to tell me twice. I shot to the bed like a rocket, but then stopped dead in my tracks.

"Hey, wait a second…Is it Easter? How'd the Easter Bunny know I'd be here!?"

Earl looked uncomfortable. "Yeah, uh…Easter was las' week, li'l man."

At that moment I realized something major was happening in my life. Easter had passed and I hadn't even known it. The sadness that filled my heart was sharp and deep. I was much too young to understand the implications of what it meant not to have a family, to lose everything, but I was smart enough to understand my life would never be the same. I grabbed the Easter basket, marched it over to the open window, and threw it out.

"This is NOT from the Easter Bunny! I don't want it! I want my mommy and I want to go home!" I threw myself on top of my bed, buried my face in the hard pillow that smelled of bleach, and cried great gasping sobs. The exhaustion of processing everything that was happening overwhelmed me. I'd never been that tired before. Earl stayed by my side on his knees on the chilly, hard linoleum floor until I slept. I was so scared that I tried to fight falling asleep. My eyes would shut, but the second I felt sleep coming I would jolt my head up to make sure Earl was still there. Earl didn't say anything. He just rubbed my back and made a very soft *"shhhhh"* sound. I didn't let sleep take me until I was sure Earl would not leave me alone.

The following morning, I woke to the sound of what seemed like a million kids. My room was filled with boys my age running around and shouting. Most of the boys were Black, but there were some Hispanic boys in the mix as well. I was the only white kid. Even with all of the commotion, I felt more alone than I ever had before. I looked at the floor and watched my feet dangle from the side of the bed as I would learn to do whenever I felt small. I wondered where Earl was.

As I was staring at the floor and my swinging toes, I saw another pair of little feet enter my field of view.

"Hi! I'm Peter!"

"Uh…I'm Gino."

When I worked up the courage to look up, I saw a little Black boy who seemed to be around my age smiling at me from under a fluffy Afro.

"I saw you last night, but Earl made us all be real quiet 'cuz you was sleepin.'"

From that moment on, Peter and I were fast friends. He had a sensitive nature, much like my own. He introduced me to the other boys and showed me where the bathroom and dining hall were. I'd never been in a communal shower before. As the only white kid, I was nervous. Even at five, boys notice their differences.

As we entered the shower, Peter showed me where to drop my pajamas. I remember feeling a little strange about taking them off, as they were now the only clothing I had. We threw them into a huge basket with everyone else's. I followed Peter's lead, then showered as fast as I could. When I was finished, I came out to find the big basket with all the pajamas was gone. I stood there naked and shivering as the older boys walked by me without saying a word. When Peter appeared after what seemed like an eternity, he asked me what I was doing. I told him I was waiting for him to finish. Peter laughed at me and told me to follow him. Around the corner from where I had been standing was where the towels were kept. I don't think I'd ever been so happy to see a towel before.

When I finished drying off, I stood there with my towel wrapped around me twice, feeling stupid.

"Uh…now what?" I asked. Peter laughed at me again and said we had to go get our clothes for the day. I followed Peter to a long line of boys of all ages wearing towels. When we reached our turn in the line, we were at the entrance to a huge closet. To my delight, we were greeted by Earl.

"Hey there, little guy. Looks like you met my boy, Peter." I smiled for the first time since the police arrived at my friend's house.

"How you doin', li'l guy?"

"Okay, I guess." It struck me again that someone so large, and a man, at that, could make me feel so safe.

"You have any problems, you come see Earl and those problems will go away. Deal?" Earl was down on his knees again and looking me right in the eyes.

"Deal!" I said, smiling from ear to ear. From that day on I was "little guy," and Peter was "my boy." We were the only two kids Earl gave nicknames. Although I saw the older boys pick on the little ones quite often, I never had a problem. No one bothered me and Peter.

The daily process of getting our clothes was awkward at first and took some getting used to. Inside the giant closet to the right were socks and underwear. To the left hung pants, shorts, and belts. Opposite the entrance to the closet hung shirts, sweaters, sweatshirts, and jackets. Shoes were organized in tight rows by size on locking racks just outside the closet door. What you wore that day depended on what fit and what was left by the time your turn came up. Sometimes we had to wear underwear or shoes that were several sizes too big. At the end of the day, we showered again and followed the same process to get our pajamas.

School was on site for the little kids, while the bigger kids were bussed to a local public school. Meals were at set times. Deviation from the schedule was not tolerated. If one kid was missing, we all waited. At the end of the meal, any kid that could walk was expected to help clean up—no exceptions.

There was one TV in the entire place. The TV room was to the left of the main staircase and was the biggest room I'd ever seen. Inside the room were dozens of metal folding chairs lined up in rows facing the TV, which hung on the wall. On the other side of the room was a pool table and a ping-pong table. It was an unspoken rule that the TV room was for the big kids, who were terrifying to me. I avoided the TV room as if it were a bear's den, but I was always impressed by it.

Peter was my constant companion. For some reason we were drawn to one another. It turned out we were nearly the same age. Thanks to Peter, I started to settle into a routine and was able to adapt. The stability and repetition at the Pink Palace were a welcome relief from the life of wondering where my mother was and how I was going to eat. Even so, my heart ached for my mother. I desperately missed her and every day I wondered if she was okay.

I have no idea how long I was at the Pink Palace. I transitioned into a regular routine with Peter by my side. The days blended into a monotonous but safe haze in which I was numb, if not truly happy. It might have lasted weeks or months, but it couldn't last forever.

If, in reading this, the Pink Palace seems more like it was a prison than a childcare facility, that's because it embodied the fundamental problem with the foster system: the cure is almost as bad as the disease. The trauma of losing one's family, particularly at an early age, often causes behavioral and developmental issues which can only be overcome by boundless patience and compassion. In a system stretched to the limits of its budget and beyond, even for those possessing these traits, it's impossible to reach every child. Instead, the system banks on sheer, monotonous consistency and institutional living, much like a prison. But consistency only numbs. It doesn't heal. Much like the convict that goes back to a life of crime upon release because that's all he knows, many kids in the system go right back to damaging behaviors when they are forced to leave.

The other side effect of this approach is a deep sense of self-blame. If you are treated like a prisoner, you come to believe, on a very deep level, you did something to deserve it. The sense of original sin, of being "less than" other kids, is instilled early. This damaging trend is compounded by the third layer of trauma: abuse by foster parents and the other children in their care.

CHAPTER 3

A Common Experience

The serious woman told me they had found an emergency foster home. I'd be leaving in the morning. Peter and I were devastated. In the middle of the night, he came to my bed and told me he didn't want me to go. We cried and I asked him if he wanted to sleep with me that night. He crawled into my bed, and we fell asleep together. When they found us in the morning, there was quite a bit of commotion among the adults. What they didn't understand was that Peter and I were like brothers, two scared little boys trying to comfort one another in the face of the unknown.

I was taken away later that morning by a social worker I can barely remember. I can only remember Peter. He stood in the driveway with tears in his eyes. I knelt facing backward and watched his Afro disappear through the car's rear window. I never saw him or Earl again. I don't know what became of them, but I will always remember Earl for his kindness. I wonder where he moved next or how many other lives he touched with his gentle soul.

My memory of the year after I left the Pink Palace is hazy. I bounced around between foster home placements, some manageable, some difficult, some horrific. I rarely stayed with any of them for more than a month. Although I don't remember many of the specifics from this time, these few months were when I developed some of the coping and defense mechanisms that would get me through the rest of my childhood.

Here, my story bounces around as well. The incident that follows happened a couple years later when I was about eight, but it demonstrates all that was wrong with the system at the time. Foster parents were not properly vetted, and abuse was rampant. Things have changed a lot since then with regards to who is allowed to be a foster parent, but kids still face abuse from other traumatized children today, and the effects are the same.

They had found me a placement in a small community called Camp Meeker on the California coast, just past Occidental. This new house was perched on the side of a mountain and was surrounded by redwood trees.

When we arrived at the door, I was greeted by a bombastic and excitable woman named Rachel.

"Oh, Gino, we are so happy you're here! How are you, dear?"

I was still reeling from my sudden and unexpected removal from my last home, but I managed a polite, "I'm okay, thank you."

My social worker and I followed Rachel into the kitchen. My hypervigilance went into immediate overdrive.

By this time, I had honed my observational skill to minute details. This unconscious practice has both haunted and helped me throughout my life. The moment I enter a room, a house, or any new and unfamiliar environment, I scan the space and the people in it. I watch body language and movement. Mannerisms, volume, and tone of voice are all carefully and methodically dissected. Furniture, fabrics, colors, temperature, and especially smells are all processed. I pay specific attention to the initial greeting; do they look me in the eyes? When they shake my hand, are they firm and steady, or does their hand and wrist go limp? This catalogue of sensory information is all processed in an instant to assess whether I am safe or whether the situation could go sour and turn violent. It's an innate habit common to kids in the system, an ongoing and exhausting gut check that my therapist assigned a name to many years later: hypervigilance.

All the internal alarms and whistles fine-tuned by previous foster experiences were now telling me to run as far and as fast as I could. I sat down, paralyzed in fear as my social worker went through the now-familiar ritual of pleasant greetings and viewing the house, which almost always started with cookies and milk in the kitchen. I ate one to be polite, but my stomach was in knots.

Rachel's husband, Richard, came in from the deck while we were sitting in the kitchen. He was jolly-looking with a short beard and reminded me of a brown-haired Santa—suspenders and all. His presence settled my internal alarms a little because he struck me as a trustworthy and sincere man. Much like Earl at the Pink Palace, he had a booming voice.

"Well, what's goin' on in here, Mother?"

Rachel smiled up at her husband and introduced me.

"You wanna see the place, Gino?" Richard asked.

"Sure," I said, forcing dry cookie down my throat.

"Pa, why don't you show Gino his room so us ladies can visit for a little bit?"

He reached out and took my hand. "Come on, Gino. Let's you and me go take a tour of your new digs."

Richard took me out the same door he had come in, which opened out to a narrow concrete staircase down the hill hugging the outside of the house.

"Now this is gonna take a little gettin' used to 'cuz when it rains these here stairs get real slippy-slidy."

I was confused. I thought we were going to my new room. I didn't understand why we were outside picking our way down the steps.

Once we got to the bottom of the slip-n-slide stairs, Richard took me through another door and into a cavernous basement room set into the hill under the house. The air was damp and frigid. I must have shivered because Richard told me it warmed up a lot when the heater was on. I said nothing. Fluorescent lights reflected off the speckled, off-white linoleum floor that stretched across the expanse between walls of painted cinderblock. There were two twin beds opposite the door, both with the same blue polyester bedspreads that had been on my bed in the Dependent Unit. On the bed to the far left of the room sat a stuffed killer whale with a red bow on it. Richard pointed to the bed and said, "I wasn't sure what to get you, so I went with what I liked when I was your age. Whenever we get a new kid, I go out and buy 'em a stuffed animal."

I was always happy to add to my collection of stuffed animals, which were a common gift upon entering a new home. I welcomed the stuffed whale as a much-needed distraction. I scooped it up and carried it along as Richard led me around the rest of the bottom floor, which featured another bedroom off a long hall and a bathroom. The sumptuous bedroom was decorated in bright pinks, blues, and purples. Richard told me that was their daughter, Rachel's, room. Rachel and Mother had the same name.

As we were going out the door, I asked Richard who slept in the other twin bed in my room. He told me Michael slept there. Rachel and Michael would be home soon, and I'd "get" to meet them, as if meeting other kids wasn't my least favorite part of entering a new foster home.

The social worker and Rachel were just finishing up as Richard and I reappeared in the doorway. By now it was pouring rain and we were soaked from coming up the stairs. Seeing me dripping on the floor, Rachel made a scowl, grabbed a kitchen towel off the counter, and threw it at me so I could dry off. The alarm bells were deafening now.

Rachel Jr. and Michael came home just as my social worker was leaving. The second I laid eyes on Rachel Jr., I knew she was trouble. I guessed she was ten or eleven, whereas I was about eight. Manicured ringlets framed her chubby face and were topped with a massive pink bow. Her dress and shoes were a matching shade of pink. She peered at me through Coke-bottle glasses, scrunching up her face, before screaming, "HI! I'M RACHEL!! MAMMA SAYS YOU GOT THE BOOT FROM YOUR LAST HOME SO THAT'S WHY YOU'RE HERE."

I recoiled as she thrust her hand in my face.

"Gino! Don't be rude! Rachel isn't going to bite you! Take her hand," admonished her mother. I did as I was told. Rachel Jr. curtsied and barked, "CHARMMM-NDA!"

Mother beamed at this introduction and asked Rachel Jr. if she wanted cookies. This was apparently the magic word. I was forgotten in an instant, and Rachel Jr. flounced into the kitchen in a whirl of fat and frills.

I was left alone in the living room with the other boy, Michael. He was small and knew how to make himself smaller. He had uncombed sandy blond hair, brown eyes, and looked about my age. His thin frame swam in brown corduroy pants and an oversized shirt, and his shoes had holes at the toes. There was never any doubt who was Mother's favored child.

He reached out, shook my hand, and asked if I'd seen our room yet.

"Ya, it's cold down there," I said.

"I know, but it's not so bad when she turns the heater on in *her* room," Michael waved in the general direction of the kitchen, "and if she leaves her bedroom door open." He told me the heater in our room didn't work and never had.

In foster care, there is often a honeymoon period that lasts for the first two or three weeks with a new family. During this period, I could usually do no wrong. Allowances were made so I could ease into the new setting and get used to the house rules. This period lasted just two days with Mother.

The day before I was to return to school, Mother instructed me to take a bath before bedtime. I climbed down the outdoor staircase and made my way into the bathroom.

The room felt like a refrigerator. I turned on the water and also turned on the room's heater, which was built into the wall, before climbing into the bathtub.

Rachel Jr. shrieked from the other room, where I had seen her stuffing her face on my way down the hall.

"WHAT'S THAT? GINO? DID YOU TURN THE HEATER ON? I'M TELLIN' MAMMA! MAMMA! GINO TURNED THE HEATER ON IN THE BATHROOM!"

I ignored her, but what I didn't know was that she had an intercom in her room connected to the upstairs. I heard the upstairs door slam shut and what sounded like an elephant come banging down the stairs.

"GINO! GINO, DO YOU HAVE THE HEATER ON IN THERE?!"

I was frozen in fear. I didn't say a word or move a muscle. WHAM! The door slammed open. Mother stood red-faced in the doorway. I could almost feel what was about to happen, so I wrapped my arms around my knees and put my head down.

"GET OUT OF THAT TUB RIGHT NOW, YOUNG MAN!" I didn't move. "ARE YOU DEAF? GET OUT BEFORE I YANK YOU OUT!"

I closed my eyes and was so scared, I peed. When Mother saw the yellow cloud swirling around me, her rage reached a new peak. "WHAT THE FUCK IS THE MATTER WITH YOU? ARE YOU RETARDED? THEY DIDN'T TELL ME YOU WERE RETARDED! Rachel, they gave us a retarded one this time!"

"Really, Mamma?" Now Rachel Jr. was standing in the bathroom with her mother, looking down at me sitting in the bathtub, paralyzed in fear with a cloud of yellow still swirling around me.

"THAT'S IT, YOU FUCKING LITTLE SISSY BOY!" Mother screamed.

In one swoop she reached into the tub and grabbed me by the hair. As my body began to lift from the tub, the pain of my hair leaving my scalp shot through me like a lightning bolt. I started to scream, which seemed to please Mother.

"GET THE FUCK OUT HERE!"

She threw me through the bathroom door while holding on to my hair. I landed on my face on the linoleum floor of the hallway in a dripping, naked heap. As I started to get up, I saw a pool of blood on the floor and panicked.

Before I could get my senses back, I saw a giant hand coming at me out of the corner of my eye. The sting of Mother's palm hitting the side of my face overtook all of my senses. I went limp as my head hit the floor again. I was far too small to defend myself, so I just accepted the fact I was going to die.

A few moments passed. I realized I was still alive but struggled to breathe and couldn't move my arms or my legs. As I opened my eyes and looked up, I saw a blurry outline of Mother sitting on top of me and pinning my arms down.

She had gotten ahold of herself and no longer sounded angry. She was doing her best to sound calm and soothing.

"It's okay, Gino, let it out. I know your inside hurts, honey, just let it go."

"WHAT ARE YOU TALKING ABOUT!?" I screamed up at her. "LET ME GO!"

I was so scared I peed again. In my current position on my back with Mother sitting on top of me, it hit her square in the back. I took some satisfaction in that.

I felt someone holding down my legs as well and managed to get a glimpse of who it was—Pa, her enabler. He looked like a deer in headlights. I kicked and spit and screamed for as long as I could. My efforts were in vain. I was much too small to be able to take on two grown adults, but I did get some perverse joy from the fact that it took two of them to hold me down.

During the entire episode, Rachel Jr. stood off to the side with a grin on her face.

When I had exhausted myself, Mother got up and barked something to Pa about putting me in my bed. The next thing I remember, it was morning. Pa was waking me up to get ready for my first day of school. I wasn't stupid enough to try to take a bath first. I got dressed and climbed up the stairs. Mother was standing in the kitchen with an apron on. As I came in, she smiled down at me and said, "Are we feeling better this morning? We'll discuss your punishment for last night when you get home from school." Punishment? As if being thrown through the air by my hair and knocked out wasn't punishment enough for being so bold as to think I could turn on the heater.

Mother took us all to school that morning, which I came to learn was a rarity. Rides to school meant Michael or I had gotten in trouble and there was a visible mark on us. The previous night had left me with a fat, cracked lip and a black eye. Mother took me into the office to get me registered, and the lady at the front desk looked horrified when she saw me. Mother took her look in stride, announcing I was one of her new foster children.

"Someone had a temper tantrum last night."

The lady behind the desk gave her a look of pained understanding, as if to say, "Oh, he's one of those. You are such a good person for taking in these pitiful children." In that moment I knew all I could do was try to stay out of Mother's sights. It wouldn't matter if I came to school beaten to a bloody pulp. It would always be my fault. No one would do anything about it.

Although this was one of the worst instances of abuse in my young childhood, it was far from an isolated incident. In more recent times, there has been a shift toward placing kids with relatives if at all possible. Strangers are now a last resort. Extensive training is also available for foster parents. They are given clear guidelines on what to expect, should they decide to foster a child. I think it would be naïve, however, to assume abuse never happens within the system anymore.

This instance also illustrates another major issue that still remains in the foster care system today. Kids often have little recourse or believability in instances of abuse. Acting out may take the form of false reporting. It's difficult for adults to tell when their stories are real or made up. I learned quickly that nothing good ever came of speaking up.

CHAPTER 4

Acting Out

Although Mother and Pa were the first foster parents I remember, they weren't the first I was placed with. I didn't go to live with them until several years after I left the Pink Palace. I don't remember my first few placements, but I do remember the fear that was instilled from them.

At six, toward the end of my first year in foster care, I was told I would be returning to the Dependent Unit. When I asked what that was, I was told I had been there once before. *It must be the Pink Palace. That's where Earl and Peter are!* My spirits soared at the prospect of seeing them again.

As we were driving, my social worker told me the Dependent Unit had moved into a brand-new building. I wasn't impressed. I liked routine. When things stayed the same, I knew what to expect. After my experiences of the past year, "new" meant unknown, scary, and not to be trusted.

The day I arrived for my second stay at the Dependent Unit, it was raining. Drops pattered off the roof of the car as it rolled down a long driveway lined with tall trees. Through the swish-swish of the windshield wipers, I could make out a huge white building. I was sure that was where we were going, but instead the car turned left and drove on. All I could see over the top of the front seat were pastures dotted here and there with placid cows weathering the rain. Just as it looked like we were about to drive off the road and into the pastures, we turned again. This is when I got my first glimpse of the new Dependent Unit. It looked nothing like the Pink Palace. The exterior was white and brown stucco with a steep, slanted roof. All the windows were a dark smoky color that made it impossible to see inside. There was no serious lady to greet us. There was no one outside at all. It looked all the more ominous in the rain. I shivered and clutched a stuffed animal from my collection—a remnant from a home that hadn't worked out.

Inside, we were met by a pretty young woman with fire-red hair.

"My name is Margaret," she said. "I'm your new social worker."

Seeing I had already retreated into stoic silence, she knelt down to my level.

"You okay?"

I shrugged. "Uh-huh."

"I think you'll like it here, Gino. There are lots of kids and toys to play with…"

She continued on, but I wasn't listening. I'd heard this speech before many times. I had learned from past experience that when an adult started giving the "You'll like it here" speech, it often meant the opposite.

The inside of the new Dependent Unit could not have been more different from the Pink Palace. As we entered the translucent glass door into the receiving office, the serious lady was still nowhere to be seen. Instead, it was as if we had stepped into a doctor's waiting room. In front of us was a tall counter with a very pleasant smiling young woman behind it. Margaret motioned for me to sit on one of the chairs lining the wall. These chairs were nothing like the chairs in the Pink Palace. They were still the bland brown of a '70s institution but were much nicer to sit on, with cushions and everything. I assumed my customary position of watching my feet dangle back and forth off the side of the chair while Margaret spoke to the smiling lady behind the desk. When she was finished, she came and sat next to me.

"Okay, Gino, I have to go now, but she's going to take you and get you all ready, okay?"

I did my best to smile back. Margaret gave me a hug and told me she'd return soon to see how I was doing.

The smiling lady walked Margaret out—and then locked the door behind her. I could feel my heart beat faster and my palms sweat. I wondered if I was going to jail. I didn't know what I had done, but the feeling that all of this was happening for a reason, that I was to blame, was already instilled in my psyche.

The smiling lady offered me her hand. After some hesitation, I took it. She was a lot gentler than the serious lady had been. When she spoke to me, her voice was soft and comforting. She asked me a few questions and then looked at the garbage bag that had arrived with me. In the year I had been in foster care, I had accumulated a few personal belongings that were handed off whenever I was. These items—clothes and stuffed animals, for the most part—had arrived in a garbage bag toted by one of the officers who had brought me in. Even today, garbage bags are often used to transport the belongings of kids in foster care. The symbolism of this practice is heartbreaking and not lost on the children themselves. Today, there are a number of charities that furnish foster kids with suitcases and other luggage so they don't feel like literal garbage.

"Are those your things, Gino?"

"Uh-huh"

"Okay, well we're going to put them someplace very safe so nothing happens to them. Before we do that, we need to take a look at what you have and write everything down, okay?"

It didn't take the smiling lady very long to write down the sum total of my possessions. I was allowed to keep two items. One of them was Sparky.

Sparky was a brown and white stuffed spaniel. He never judged and had soft, sad brown eyes. Every night before I fell asleep, I'd kiss Sparky, tell him I loved him, and hold him tight. I suppose it was my way of bracing for whatever the next day might bring. I had grown accustomed to uncertainty, but Sparky was steady and loyal. Holding on to him was my way of feeling safe.

The smiling lady continued down her checklist. "Okay, now we need you to see the nurse." My mind raced with questions about why I had to see a nurse. Was I sick? I was terrified, but on the outside, I remained rigid and silent, even as my eyes welled.

I had learned to be stoic and silent, hiding my fear and sadness in an apparent lack of emotion. Fear, I had learned, was a sign of weakness. It was always the weak kids that got picked on. The effects of the trauma were still there, but I had repressed them. This process of prolonged emotional repression, especially for young kids who are still developing social and coping skills, can have devastating effects that play out throughout their lives. I was no exception.

The smiling lady knocked on a door that was paneled in dark wood with a peephole at the top.

"Sandy? I have our newest guest, Gino, here. He's ready for you now."

I heard the door unlock and it swung open to reveal a young woman who smelled of cornmeal. Perhaps it was the cornstarch in her gloves or the starch in her uniform, but I still associate her with that smell.

"Well! Aren't you just too cute!?" she blurted out, putting her hands on her knees to get a better look at me. My head dropped and I gazed at the floor.

"Thanks," I mumbled as the smiling lady handed me off to the cornstarch lady and walked out. Now that we were alone, it took everything I had to fight back my tears.

"Uh—am I sick? Is this a hospital?" I asked. "I thought I was going back to the Dependent Unit! Do I have to get a shot? Are you going to cut my hair?" The questions flew out in a gush. My body began to shake uncontrollably, and I could feel the tears coming again.

Sensing my panic, the cornstarch lady got down on her knees and took hold of my arms. She looked into my eyes and, with a calm and very soothing voice, said, "Gino, you're not sick and you're not in a hospital. There is nothing to be afraid of. I'm just going to look in your mouth and your ears. See this little hammer? I'm going to bounce it on your knee to see if you can kick me. We're going to give you what is called a physical."

"What's a physical?" I asked. I was six years old and had never had one before. She explained it to me. Her kindness and soothing voice put me at ease. The exam itself was over before I knew it. She did everything she had talked about but made sure to put me at ease the whole time. When we were finished, she picked up the phone, and the smiling lady reappeared.

"I hear you're all done."

I nodded, knowing what came next. "Do I have to take a shower now?"

"Yes, please. We need to make sure you're clean so you don't get sick."

The smiling lady asked if I remembered how to shower from my stay at the Pink Palace. I nodded, keeping my mouth shut and my eyes on the floor. I still remembered the smell of the soap and the heat of the water.

"Where's Earl?" I asked. Both ladies looked at one another and then looked down at me.

"Earl?" This told me all I needed to know; Earl wasn't here. They'd probably left him in the Pink Palace.

"Never mind," I said. I wondered if Earl was as alone as I was.

As I was showering and washing with the yucky soap, a familiar feeling came over me. Deep, inconsolable sadness welled up from somewhere in my stomach. I was right back at the beginning. I could no longer hold back my tears. I sat on the floor of the shower and started to sob—the kind of crying that comes from deep inside and causes physical pain. I don't know how long I stayed like that, but eventually the smiling lady came to check on me.

"Are you just about done?" she asked through the curtain.

I was sobbing so deeply that no sound came out of my mouth. I could not speak.

"Hello? Gino, are you in there, honey?" I still couldn't make a sound, so I started to hit the wall. I heard the smiling lady call out to the other lady. The shower curtain flew back. I was curled up in a ball on the shower floor rocking back and forth. The smiling lady reached into the shower and scooped me up in her arms. She sat on the floor of the bathroom with me in her arms until I stopped sobbing. She didn't say a word to me, just held me in her arms and rocked back and forth. For the first time in a long while, I felt safe.

When the storm had subsided, the smiling lady asked me if I was hungry. I nodded, but I couldn't figure out how to get dressed. She asked me if I knew how to dress myself. It is not uncommon for children that have suffered abuse or neglect to be emotionally behind their peers. I was capable of dressing myself at that age, but the fear and anxiety I had been suppressing for the past year had left me helpless.

Once she had helped me into my clothes, the smiling lady took me to the kitchen and asked me to have a seat. An older woman came out of the kitchen, leaned down, smiled, and said she had heard I was hungry. She brought out some semi-warm vegetables and something like meatloaf that was gray and soggy. Having gone through the grief of crying in the shower, I was overcome with intense rage. I was not going to eat another bland, institutional meal. I was not going to start over and pretend everything would be fine. Without warning, I threw the plate across the room. I jumped out of my chair and threw my cup of milk against the wall. I was screaming and writhing on the floor in a fit of pure rage.

The smiling lady wasn't smiling anymore. She got down on the floor, wrapped her arms around me, and held me in a kind but firm bear hug. I wiggled, kicked, and screamed with every bit of strength I had in my body.

"LET ME GO! YOU'RE NOT MY MOMMY! LEAVE ME ALONE!"

The older lady joined the smiling lady in trying to hold me down, but I was shaking and punching with all I had. The older lady had to hold my feet as the smiling lady did her best to restrain my upper body, but the tighter they held, the harder I fought. Someone called out and soon a man rushed into the room to help. I screamed and writhed like an animal in a trap. It took all three of the adults to keep me from hurting them or myself. They did their best not to harm me as I raged. I remember one of them saying to me, "It's okay, Gino. Let it out. You're going to be okay."

After nearly half an hour, the fit passed as quickly as it had arrived. I was exhausted. There was no more fight left in me. The man that had joined the fray scooped me up and carried me away. He took me down the boy's hall to a large bedroom, placed me in a bed, and sat down next to me. We didn't say a word, but he stroked my hair and it wasn't long before I fell asleep.

Fits of rage, deep sorrow, and "acting out" were to be a theme in my childhood. One that would undermine many would-be foster placements. Abuse builds in the body like a toxin. Because I couldn't release it while in the abusive situation, it fell to those who cared and had good intentions to bear the brunt of the emotions I had suppressed for months or years. Many were not ready for this reality. They saw themselves as rescuers of adorable children without the understanding they were bringing a ticking time bomb into their homes; that the very feeling of comfort and safety they were proud to provide was the catalyst that caused long-dormant emotions to explode.

This is still true today. There is much more training available to prepare for the effects of compounded repressed trauma that is the norm for foster kids, but training is one thing and reality is another. The more trauma kids have, the more they act out. The more they act out, the less likely it is for them to find a permanent family and the more they bounce around in the system collecting trauma. It's a vicious cycle of rejection, rage, and self-blame that takes a special combination of love, structure, and support to unravel.

As another form of acting out, I continued to express myself in feminine ways by dancing around like a princess. I learned that in rural Northern California in the late '70s, this behavior made adults uncomfortable, and since it wasn't disruptive or dangerous, they weren't sure how to react. It was as much a way to fight back against my situation as it was an expression of a sexual identity not yet discovered.

Other kids acted out in different ways. Some screamed. Some abused their peers. Some were violent. Some even spread their own feces on the walls, which was considered to be one of the worst indicators of psychological trauma, second only to killing animals. It was a behavior I only encountered a couple of times, but it was like a black spot on the record, an indicator the child was too damaged to ever find a permanent home.

The rest of my memory about my second stay at the Dependent Unit is a bit fuzzy. I remember the beds were a little better than the ones at the Pink Palace, long hallways of rooms, one for the girls and one for the boys, and a larger TV room. There was even a playground with a jungle gym. For the first time, I was bussed to a public school, but I was only there a few months before I was moved again.

CHAPTER 5

The Importance of Stability

From the Dependent Unit, I was transferred to a group home in Novato, which was run by an organization called Children's Garden. This home had been started as part of a foundation by a trio of celebrities. It was meant to be a temporary home, but like the Dependent Unit, it ended up becoming a long-term refuge for kids awaiting adoption or possible reunification with their birth parents. At this time, there was much less understanding or training around how to deal with childhood trauma than is available today. Raising deeply troubled children was a task the first House Parents were ill prepared for. It was only through the sheer force of dedication, patience, and emotional fortitude that they blazed a trail which led the home to become recognized as the premier model for excellence upon which others in the state would be based.

My stay at Children's Garden was the longest I had ever spent anywhere. I remember the day I arrived in bits and pieces.

The rest of the children were at school. Margaret and I were greeted by the House Parents, Shippy and Jennifer. I can still hear the gentle sound of Jennifer's voice in my head when I think of her—it was distinctive and lilting like the burble of running water. I took to her from the first time we met. Jennifer had blond hair and blue eyes, and to look at us standing side by side, one might assume she was my mother. She took me by the hand and gave me a tour of the ranch-style house, including the bedroom I would be sharing with another little boy named Eric. Then I was allowed to watch TV until the rest of the children came home.

In addition to myself, there were five children in the house, three boys and two girls, all between the ages of five and eight. Unlike the kids at the Dependent Unit, these kids welcomed me and treated me with kindness for the most part. We all sat down at the same table for dinner, which was another first for me, and had a home-cooked meal. For the first time, I had the sense of belonging to a family. My new roommate, Eric, was Hispanic with dark, almost black hair. He was very boisterous and liked the rough-and-tumble activities. Another boy was a little more reserved with sandy blond hair and blue eyes. He was in a phase of being enchanted with motor homes. He spewed endless facts about the Pace Arrow and how he'd have one when he grew up. Another was obsessed with everything about the Empire State Building. This kind of passion or interest was foreign to me. Up until then, I had never been in one place long enough to think beyond the immediacy of my circumstances. I had my stuffed animals and that was it.

There was also a girl named Una who scared me from the moment I met her. I could tell something was very off about her. She was a large child with thick glasses who bullied the rest of us whenever she got the chance. I made it a point not to be alone with her, but there were times it couldn't be avoided. When she did get me alone, she would order me to touch her. She never touched me, but this was my first introduction to sex and female anatomy that I understood. She never forced me, but it still didn't feel normal.

When a child is sexually abused at an early age, it is very common for that child to reach out for what they perceive as love when interacting with other children. As I look back now, I can't imagine what Una must have already experienced in her young life that gave her the idea there was no way to give or receive love other than by using her body. None of us thought much of it at the time. We were just kids coping the best we could.

This is another danger inherent in the system. Even though parents are now much more stringently vetted and go through rigorous training, abuse can come from other foster children within the home who are expressing their own trauma through violence.

Despite Una's bullying, my first few months at Children's Garden are some of the happiest memories I have. For the first time in my life, I could just play.

Jennifer had a beautiful singing voice and used to sing to all of us. I loved the sound of her voice. During my first few months there, we all went to a recording studio and made a record. The proceeds from the album went to support Children's Garden. It was a small 45 LP with one song on each side. The A-side featured a song Jennifer had written. She led all of us to sing it together. I was chosen to do a solo for the B-side of the album. I still have a copy of the record in my house and still remember the lyrics.

> *There once was a garden*
> *A very special garden*
> *of children*
> *A garden of growing children filled*
> *with heartbreak and sorrow*

I have not listened to it in fifteen years.

Jennifer's beautiful voice made an intense impression on me. Many years later, as a young adult living in Santa Barbara and working at Nordstrom, I had my head down helping a customer when I heard someone speaking in line and knew it was her. I whipped around and picked her out of the jumble of people.

"Jennifer?"

She turned and saw me, but I could tell by the confusion on her face she didn't know who I was. Without thinking, I started singing the song...

"There once was a garden. A very special garden..."

Tears welled up in her eyes as she stepped over to my counter.

"Gino?"

I came out from behind the counter and hugged her. To this day, she still holds a place in my heart as one of the kindest people I encountered on my journey.

Just a few months after my arrival at the Children's Garden, my stable world threatened to come crashing down again. Shippy and Jennifer sat us all down and announced they would be leaving. They would be there for two more weeks. Then we would get new House Parents.

I stared at my feet and said nothing. For the next two weeks, my silence continued. I did not interact with the other kids and stayed clear of Shippy and Jennifer. Their last day was one of the worst days I had experienced since the day the police took me from my birth mother. I clung to Jennifer's leg screaming and crying for her not to leave me. Jennifer did her best to comfort me, but I could not be consoled. As I watched them drive away in their Winnebago, I felt lost, abandoned, and alone. I didn't know it at the time, but the next couple of years would be among the most stable and healthy periods of my childhood.

The new House Parents were named Kathy and Leo. They had been two broke hippies who responded to an ad in the paper for the job. They had no formal training and no idea what it meant to be in charge of six traumatized kids, but somehow, through sheer will and some kind of magic, they made it work. Now, looking back as an adult, I can see and appreciate all Kathy and Leo did for me in the two years I lived under their care.

Kathy was a tall, slender woman with dark, flowing hair that reminded me of my birth mother. To me, she epitomized '70s glamour. She always wore a gold chain with a large gold pendant hanging from it. Leo was a stout, masculine man with a full beard and a mane of dark brown curly hair. Both spoke with a thick East Coast accent from New York or New Jersey. They remained the House Parents for the next two and a half years I was there.

Many of my firsts were with Kathy and Leo. The first time I can remember catching a bad case of the flu, I was so sick that I passed out on the way home from school. I was brought home by the police. I remember Kathy coming and going from my sick room with cold compresses and soothing words. It was my first experience with true maternal love and nurturing.

Leo taught me how to ride a bike. I went on my first family vacation with them, my first camping trip, and learned to spell my first word. I learned routine was not the best life had to offer. With Kathy and Leo there was comfort, love, and safety for the first time—and more than that, a sense of belonging.

Christmases were like a dream come true. Each year Children's Garden had a Christmas party. The organization had several homes scattered around Marin County, and every Christmas they all came together to celebrate the holiday. I had never seen so many presents!

I learned, through many, many temper tantrums, how to express anger and frustration in socially appropriate ways. The family environment helped create a sense of trust that allowed me to deal with some of the atrocities of my past. In addition to the structure and discipline, intense psychotherapy was provided, although I'm not sure the therapists knew how to deal with us either. We would intentionally mess with them as yet another form of acting out.

I still suffered from fits of rage. There were times I would lose all control, requiring Leo to restrain me so I didn't hurt myself. While I would scream and pound the floor in blind rage, Kathy would soothe me with gentle words while Leo pressed his fist into my stomach. This was not to hurt me. The sensation somehow helped me return to myself. Over time, I gained the ability to master my emotions to a much greater extent.

It was also during this time that the concept of adoption became real to me as a possibility. Until then, I had some sense other kids led very different lives, but I had never even considered long-term normalcy as a possibility for me.

It all started when we were told Eric would be leaving; an adoptive home had been found for him. I remember being delighted for him, but it also meant my new family would be changing. I knew there would be another boy replacing him as my roommate, a kid I would be expected to treat as a member of the family. I announced I did not want to share my room with the new kid and was allowed to move into my own room in the house.

And then it happened. I came home from school, and Eric was gone. Several weeks passed and all the children anxiously awaited the news of the new kid who would replace Eric—all except me. I didn't want anyone else. I was happy with the way things had been. If I couldn't have Eric in the family, then I didn't want some replacement kid. When Kathy and Leo sat us all down and said a new little boy would be joining our family by the end of the week, I didn't participate in the rapid, excited questioning the other kids rattled off. Instead, I said nothing and stared at my feet. My reticence was not lost on Kathy and Leo. They tried their best to comfort me, but I had gone back into survival mode with the upset of my new order. I was dreading Friday, the day the new kid was going to arrive. I had already made up my mind I was going to hate him.

CHAPTER 6

Found Family

As I walked home from school on Friday afternoon, I was devising a plan of attack against my new nemesis. I made sure to take my time, so I was the last one home. When I got to the house, I took a deep breath, turned the knob, and got ready to square off with the intruder before I walked in the front door.

I slammed my backpack on the pile with the rest of the packs, took off my jacket, and stormed into the living room. Just as I was preparing the iciest of receptions, I stopped with my mouth open and my eyes wide. Over the back of the living room couch, I caught sight of a very familiar puff of dark hair. My tough-guy plan evaporated. I ran around to confirm what was too good to be true…

"Peter!!! What are you doing here?!"

He looked up at me with the same sad, confused look I had had back at the Pink Palace. He had no idea who I was.

"Peter," I said. "It's me, Gino!" I grabbed him in a tight embrace, and he hugged me back.

Kathy and Leo exchanged a confused look.

The new kid, still hugging me, said, "Hi, I'm C.C."

It turned out it wasn't Peter at all, just someone who looked like him, but it didn't matter. I had already determined in my mind that he was my brother from the Pink Palace. For his part, C.C. was not about to turn down such an enthusiastic ally in this strange new home. We alternated between hugging one another and jumping up and down with excitement.

Everyone else in the room was shocked. Kathy and Leo had feared the worst for our meeting, but they needn't have bothered. My intricate plan of attack against my new nemesis had been a waste of time, a lesson that even if things have been bad in the past, losing faith and obsessing over the worst-case scenario is often a lot of trouble for nothing.

I still remember that as one of the happiest moments of my young life. Up until recently, I could have sworn it was C.C. who was with me in the Pink Palace, but in the end, it didn't matter. We were inseparable as brothers from that moment forward and forged a bond closer than blood. For a child growing up without family, finding someone with whom you share something essential is a feeling for which there are no words.

Within a week, we had convinced Kathy and Leo to let us share a room. C.C. fit in well at school. At first, I was even jealous of him because everyone liked him so much, but I soon learned there were big benefits to having him as my brother and best friend. I was never interested in playing sports at recess, instead preferring the monkey bars, hopscotch, or jumping rope. This gave the other boys ammunition to torment me, as did my feminine presentation and movement, but C.C. wouldn't have it. More than once he stood up for me.

Even though I was becoming much more emotionally stable, I would still act out by dressing in a more feminine way or dancing around with a shirt on my head because I knew it made the adults, especially Leo, uncomfortable. C.C.'s way of acting out was running away. He never got very far, but he had to be watched constantly. Often the cops were sent out looking for him. He was also stubborn and defiant. When told to stand in the corner until he felt he had learned his lesson, he would stand there all day in defiance. When he was done, though, I'd be there to comfort him.

Each of the other kids had behavioral issues as well. We were often taken for visits and trial periods with prospective new parents, but always returned within a week or two as we tested the relationships and found, good intentions or not, they always failed.

It's hard to describe the mixed feelings of guilt and happiness knowing your brothers and sisters have been denied a lifelong home, but also that you have them back in your life. As a cute, white, blond boy with blue eyes, I was taken for many trial periods during this time, but I was always happy when the inevitable day came when I was returned to the Children's Garden and C.C. was there waiting.

For C.C. as a little Black child, there weren't any trial visits. This is how I came to learn about racism at a young age. Likewise, C.C. learned about what it meant to be gay. Not that we discussed it, but we knew something was different about each of us and how others saw us on a fundamental level.

The other kids on the block and in the schoolyard knew we were from the group home and were "problem kids." Couple this with my not-so-latent sexuality and C.C.'s small stature and skin color, and we were often at the bottom of the playground totem pole. There were always fights, but we had each other. If anyone messed with one of us, the other would jump in without a moment's hesitation.

C.C. had been through seven foster homes before arriving at Children's Garden and had suffered intense abuse. Whenever one or the other of us was having a temper tantrum that was so severe it required that we be restrained, the other would sit off to the side in silence while Kathy talked us through it and Leo held us down like a human straitjacket.

When the temper tantrum was over, C.C. would take my hand or I would take his, and we would go off together. Sometimes I would hear him screaming, drop whatever I was doing, and come running. I would sit patiently and wait for it to pass so I could be there for him afterward. It was this bond that taught me how to form strong, life-long connections with people. Even as I sit here writing about him, I can feel the strength of the love we share. I still take a moment to remember him on his birthday each year.

Both our young lives had been filled with so much loss and sadness that we were able to appreciate—even at six years old—how fortunate we were to have been brought together. We spent hours riding our bikes and just being goofy. We put cards in the spokes and pretended we were motorcycle cops—partners to the end like Jon and Ponch on *CHiPs* (although I secretly yearned to be Wonder Woman instead, with her fabulous collection of beautiful outfits). We also watched shows like *The Facts of Life* and *Diff'rent Strokes*, which were both about adopted kids. These shows made us feel more normal. I never laughed so much, or so hard, as when I was with C.C.

A few times over the course of the summer, Kathy and Leo would load a battered camper into the bed of their pickup. We would pack it full of marshmallows and sleeping bags for a weekend of roughing it among the trees. During the drive out to the woods and back, we kids would all be crammed in the bed compartment over the truck's cab. We would run wild in the woods and sleep under the stars for a couple of days before clambering back into the camper, grubby, happy, and stuffed with hotdogs for the ride home. It was a little boy's dream come true.

On one of these trips, C.C. crawled into our tent while Kathy and Leo were working on dinner. I was there with a couple of the other kids. C.C.'s eyes darted back and forth to make sure we weren't being watched. He put a finger to his lips, opening his sweatshirt like a street hustler. Inside was a trembling ball of adorable fur. Whether through cleverness, athleticism, or a combination of the two, he had managed to capture a baby rabbit.

My eyes went wide. One of the other kids grabbed a shoebox we had brought toiletries in, dumped it out, and handed it to C.C. without a word.

That night, we whispered and giggled as we jostled for position around the shoebox in the dark. We took turns feeding the bunny pieces of lettuce we had pilfered from dinner. It was so much better than the stuffed animals I had always been surrounded with and was the beginning of my love of pets.

The next day, Kathy and Leo poked their heads into the tent to see what all the fuss had been about the night before, but we had already shifted our contraband to one of the other tents and the rabbit remained undetected.

All weekend long, we kids took turns caring for the tiny bunny until it was time to go home.

We were heartbroken at the thought of having to return it to the wild, but then someone came up with a plan. We had kept Kathy and Leo on their toes all weekend. They were too tired to notice when one kid distracted them, and others smuggled the shoebox into the back of the camper. We cuddled and cooed over it the whole way home and used the same distraction tactic to get it into the house.

Using our tent strategy of shifting the rabbit from room to room, we were able to keep our secret pet hidden for one glorious week.

Then, one day, we came home from school to find Kathy and Leo sitting in the kitchen with grim expressions and the shoebox on the table in front of them. We were all grounded, and Leo had to drive the poor rabbit all the way back to the woods to return it to the campground.

Despite occasional mischievous misadventures, Kathy and Leo started developing deeper feelings toward C.C. and me. They did their best to hide it from the other kids. Nobody likes to admit they have favorites, but I could tell by the way they spoke to us that we were special. They never flaunted their feelings in front of any of the other children. It was never spoken of, but there was a sense that Kathy, Leo, C.C., and I were a family within the larger family. I loved it.

C.C. and I often talked late at night. Sometimes, when one of us couldn't sleep because we were scared or confused, we would crawl into the other's bed and hold on tight to one another. I had wised up to how adults responded to the sight of two boys in the same bed, so we were very careful to return to our own beds before morning. This ritual never involved words. I knew when he needed me, and he knew when I needed him. There was no invitation required. Of all the treatment and behavior modification we experienced while at Children's Garden, I believe the most effective therapy came from our relationship with one another. Brotherly love forged of mutual need is powerful medicine for a damaged soul. Life at Children's Garden was my first taste of living as a normal child. I remember long summer days, birthdays, holidays, and wonderful family trips—all with C.C. by my side.

The last time I saw my birth mother as a child was also when I was at Children's Garden. I was bouncing off the walls when I heard she was coming. I hadn't seen her since I had been taken from her two years earlier. She pulled up in a white car, huge and extravagant. It was driven by an unknown man who turned out to be her third husband. He seemed nice enough and did his best to buddy up to me, but I ignored him. I was only interested in Jackie.

On a rack on the back of the car was a new bike. It was yellow and black with a sparkling black banana seat. My eyes lit up when I saw it. Jackie was just stepping out of the car when I threw my arms around her. It seems sad in hindsight, but I knew she wasn't there to take me back and I was glad. The Children's Garden had become my home—a more stable home than she had ever been able to provide.

She only stayed the one afternoon. I remember her telling me I would be coming home with her soon, but it didn't bother me because I knew it wasn't true. She also told me her mother—my favorite grandmother, Lucille—had died. The news hit me like a freight train. I could still remember Lucille's laugh and how she called me "Binky" while chasing me around the house. She had made me feel loved. Now I felt as though another tie to familial permanence was severed.

Before Jackie and her new husband left, she knelt down and hugged me for a long time. She told me she would see me soon and couldn't wait to show me my new room. She had tears in her eyes as she walked out the door with me in tow. I watched as her husband helped her—now sobbing—into the car. I was sad watching them drive away, not because I wasn't leaving with her, but because she was sad. I felt ashamed of my anxiety surrounding even the possibility of returning to life with her. I need not have worried. I never went home and did not see my birth mother again until I was nearly sixteen years old.

Not long after Jackie's visit, my social worker, Margaret, sat down at the kitchen table with me, Kathy, and Leo. She told me a judge had decided it would be better for me to be placed in an adoptive home. They had kept me at the Children's Garden a long time in hopes that Jackie could pull her life together enough to get custody again, but it just hadn't happened.

I was consumed with conflicting emotions. Fear, excitement, sadness, and a tremendous sense of remorse came over me as I was told I would never return to my birth mother, but if I was adopted, I would *finally* have a place to call home. I found myself struggling with the thought of leaving C.C. I knew the likelihood of us being reunited was small indeed. Being approved for adoption was another experience we shared. About the same time I was freed for adoption, C.C. was too.

Margaret also told me I would be getting a new social worker. Her name was Jay. She was with State Adoptions. Jay was a petite, slender woman who spoke with a strong East Indian accent and drove a dark maroon Mercedes station wagon that I considered the height of luxury. During one visit, she showed me a picture of myself that had been put in a magazine. This was prior to the internet, so pictures of children that were available for adoption were printed in a booklet. I remember thinking how cool it was that I was "famous." Looking back as an adult, I am filled with heartache. I now see that pamphlet as what it was—a human version of the pound.

It wasn't long after meeting Jay that I was called into another kitchen meeting. Kathy, Leo, and C.C. sat down with me. I remember Kathy having tears in her eyes and C.C. grinning from ear to ear. Kathy and Leo told me they would be leaving Children's Garden. C.C. would be going with them because they were going to adopt him. I didn't understand. Why didn't they want me too?

It wasn't until years later that I learned the truth. It takes a while to process adoption papers. When Kathy and Leo made the decision to adopt months earlier, there was still a chance, however small, that my birth mother could win me back. Even if she didn't, my chances of finding a home were pretty good, even with my waning behavior problems.

C.C., as a Black boy, would have been left to grow up in the system. I've never blamed Kathy and Leo for making the decision to take him, not even then. Somehow, I knew he needed them more. I was just sad to lose my brother.

Just as Shippy and Jennifer had done, Kathy and Leo began making their transition out of the family. This time, I was much calmer and more grounded. Although the disruption was upsetting, the tireless work Kathy and Leo had put in over the previous two years had left me with the ability to face change with a sense of hope and inner calm. Of course, I was sad to see them go, but I also knew my time of departure was not far away. C.C. and I said our tearful goodbyes and hugged. I wondered if I would ever see him again.

The new House Parents were older, and we ran circles around them. The structured and disciplined life Kathy and Leo had worked so hard to build for us collapsed. Of course, as a kid, I loved every minute of it—until we got a visit from the head office. We were all put on restriction and had to stay in our rooms for two days.

I don't remember much else about the new parents. My adoption process began just a few weeks after their arrival. I was now almost eight years old, and for the first time in my life, a secure and permanent home felt within reach.

Jay told me there was a family interested in meeting me. They owned and operated the ferry boat that took people out to Angel Island on the San Francisco Bay. I went and stayed with them for a while. Then, out of nowhere, they changed their minds.

A few weeks later, Jay came to visit me again. This time, I was set up with another family, the Nielsons. The transition to living with the Nielsons was not an easy one. I remember feeling as if I could never do anything right. The safety I had so looked forward to never came. It seemed as if I was always in trouble for one thing or another. The Nielsons believed in spanking with a belt, and I became very familiar with the process. My frustration level rose to critical mass, and the temper tantrums that had subsided while at Children's Garden returned with a vengeance. I screamed I hated them, that they weren't my parents, and that I wanted to leave.

I was at school when I found out. I was called out of class and told to bring my things. I had an awful sinking feeling in my stomach. When I arrived at the office, I was greeted by Jay. Her downcast eyes confirmed my fears. The Nielsons had decided they could not care for me anymore. Despite all the conflicts with the Nielsons, I couldn't understand what was happening. This was supposed to be my forever family, and now I was being sent away.

Over the course of these attempted placements, I grew to see the promise of adoption as an empty one. For C.C., it had meant a stable home and caring family. For me, it was just another word for being shuffled from house to house, unwanted and unworthy.

CHAPTER 7

The Change a Little Kindness Can Make

I'm not sure why I didn't return to the Children's Garden or the Dependent Unit after the Nielsons. I think perhaps since they had started the adoption process and I was no longer a ward of the state. Somehow, I had slipped through the cracks again, and an emergency foster home had to be found until my "dependent" status could be reasserted.

Jay looked around to find me another home, and this was when I was placed with "Mother" and "Pa" in Camp Meeker, where I was beaten for turning on the heater in the bathroom.

The night after receiving the beating, Mother informed me at dinner I would be helping the camp workers in the garden all day on Saturday and Sunday. In the meantime, I would be taking my meals in my room and would not be allowed to go out and play.

Pa, the sad but dutiful enforcer, came in and got me out of bed at six o'clock Saturday morning, saying, "Sorry, Gino, but it's time to get up."

Camp Meeker was in a lush grove. Tall redwood trees and wild ferns crowded for space. The deep forest gave the camp a mysterious feel that I always loved despite my experience there. The church was located at the very edge of the camp and overlooked a beautiful valley. The property around the church was called "the garden" and was terraced into dirt lots. A path cut through the middle of the lots and descended to a ridge with unobstructed views of the valley and forest below.

Pa explained that my job was going to be to carry rocks back and forth, and he pointed to a huge pile of native rocks. The pile was at least four feet tall and ten feet wide. My jaw dropped.

"Really?"

"Yes, Gino, this is your penance."

"What's penance?"

"Penance is how you tell God that you're sorry, and the only way to prove how sorry you are is to work really hard."

This was the moment I began to believe that God did not exist.

From sunrise to sunset, I worked on the wall. When I would get too tired and felt like I was about to collapse, I was allowed to stack the smaller rocks into the wall. The larger rocks were a struggle to carry. Sometimes it took me ten minutes to drag one from the stack to where the workers were building the wall a few yards away. Once in a while, one of the workers would take pity on me and help.

By the time I got home on Saturday night, my hands were blistered and bloody and I was too tired to eat. I collapsed into my bed and didn't move until six o'clock Sunday morning—only to start all over again when Pa came and woke me up. I stumbled out of bed and into the same dirty clothes I had worn the day before. I was so sore I could barely move. I was still rubbing the sleep from my eyes as Pa and I entered the work site. Just as I had done the day before, I started hauling my rocks back and forth.

By ten in the morning, the clouds that had sheltered me the day before had burned off. The sky was clear, and the sun shone hot. I started to feel dizzy and nauseous. By eleven, I could feel my knees buckle and my stomach churn. I dropped the rock I was carrying, scurried around to the other side of the pile, and vomited violently. I felt like I was dying. The world started to spin, there was a sharp, stabbing pain on my forehead, and then everything went black.

The next thing I remember was opening my eyes to the sight of a giant man standing over me. The sun was behind him, so all I could see was his silhouette.

"Son? Son, are you okay?"

I knew this voice, but I couldn't place it.

The silhouette scooped me up and sat down on the pile of rocks with me in his arms. It was then that I got a good look at his face.

"Shippy?" I asked.

Shippy's eyes widened as he put on his glasses.

"Gino? What are you doing here?"

I felt the world shift once again for the better. "I live here now."

"Where?" Shippy asked.

"Um…with him and his wife, down the hill."

By this time Pa had come looking for me and had stumbled into my reunion. His manner and voice changed upon seeing me with Shippy.

"There you are! What happened to you, son?"

"How long has he been out here?" Shippy asked Pa.

"Well, Reverend, we started at six this morning." I couldn't figure out why Richard was calling Shippy "Reverend," but I sensed Shippy had authority here, so I took full advantage of the situation.

"That's just today," I chimed in.

"Just today?!" Shippy's brows furrowed in concern.

"And how long did you work out here yesterday?"

"I don't know," I said, "but it was dark when I got here, and it was dark when we went home."

Shippy's expression was hard as he looked at Pa.

"Gino, you go up to the house," he said. "It's over there. Jennifer will be very happy to see you. I'll be up there in a few minutes."

I made my way to the house with as much speed as my wobbling legs could muster. I rang the doorbell and knocked on the door.

"Okay, just a moment. I'm coming!" Jennifer's melodious voice, safe and soothing as always, greeted me from within. She opened the door and looked down at me as if I were a stranger.

"Well, hello there. May I help you?"

I couldn't contain my excitement. I told her Shippy had sent me, and she welcomed me in but still didn't recognize me. As I walked past her, she got a better look at me and said, "What on Earth? What happened to your head and face?"

I reached up and felt an egg-sized bump on my forehead and some dried and crusty blood. She started dabbing at my face with a warm, soft washrag. I mumbled something about hitting my head on a rock.

"That must have been some rock," she said, unconvinced. "Can I get you some milk and cookies?"

I nodded and she sent me to the bathroom to wash up. I still had a sense she didn't know who I was. When I got a look at myself in the mirror, I understood why. My hair was dirty and messy, my clothes were torn and covered in dried mud, and my face was a mask of filth and dried blood despite her ministrations.

I took some time cleaning myself up, and when I came out to the kitchen, Jennifer was at the stove with a baby in her arms.

"Where did that come from?" I asked with a hint of disgust. Jennifer turned to respond and nearly dropped the baby.

"Gino? Oh my God! What are you doing here?"

She deposited the baby in a playpen, threw her arms around me, and hugged me so hard, I could barely breathe, but for the first time since I'd left Children's Garden, my internal alarms went silent.

"Did you run away? What happened to you?"

"Uh—no, I live here now, down the hill with…"

Jennifer finished my sentence, "Richard and Rachel?"

Her face betrayed a combination of relief and concern.

"Look who I found down there working on the wall," said Shippy as he walked into the kitchen.

I wolfed down my cookies and milk so fast I almost choked. Jennifer and Shippy's house was warm and inviting, and I found myself lost in the fantasy of them coming to my rescue. For a few hours I didn't have a care in the world. Jennifer introduced me to the baby girl she had been holding when I came out of the bathroom. Her name was Abigail. She had been born not long after the couple had left the Children's Garden. I thought Abigail was the luckiest kid in the world. Then the phone rang.

I knew the moment Jennifer picked up the phone that the person at the other end of the line was Mother. When Jennifer put the phone down, the look on her face told me all I needed to know. I had to go back. My heart sank. I could tell Shippy and Jennifer didn't want to send me back either, but there was nothing they could do for the moment. As I was walking out of the house, they both hugged me tight and said I could come back anytime I wanted.

The walk home took all of five minutes. When I came in the front door, Mother was in the kitchen putting the finishing touches on dinner.

"Nice of you to show up," she said, oozing disdain. "Wash your hands. Dinner is ready." I did as I was told and didn't say a word. I could tell she hated me more than ever, and I soon found out why.

The camp at the top of the hill was a Christian camp, and Shippy was the camp's moral and spiritual leader. Almost everyone that lived at Camp Meeker attended the church, so to cross Shippy and Jennifer was to cross the community. Although I never heard another word about it, I suspect Shippy gave Pa a good tongue lashing for inflicting such a harsh and unreasonable punishment on an eight-year-old.

Mother never struck me again, but she made it very clear I meant nothing more to her than a paycheck. She yelled and screamed a lot, but that was as far as it went after that.

I have no idea how long I was with Mother and Pa, but the alarm bells never left my head. I often found myself knocking at Shippy and Jennifer's front door. Their house was the one place I felt safe. I also knew Mother didn't like it, so spending time with them was my way of turning the screws a bit.

When the end came, it started with a tea party. In Mother's eyes, Rachel Jr. was the world's most perfect child. This cast her in the role of warden over Michael and me whenever we were downstairs. When she wanted to play, we played. Her favorite activities were tea parties, and Michael and I were always conscripted as her reluctant guests.

At one of these tea parties in the bathroom downstairs, Rachel Jr. sat in the tub as if she were at a bar serving us. Michael and I sulked through the motions, paying little attention to what she was doing. As I drew my teacup to my mouth, I noticed a strange odor and the color of the "tea" didn't seem right. I took a sip, and just as I was about to swallow, Rachel Jr. screamed, "NO! You idiot! Don't drink it! I put cleanser in it as pretend sugar!"

I spit the tainted "tea" out and it hit her square in the chest.

"Now look what you did, you retard!"

She jumped out of the tub and shot down the hall and up the stairs to her mother.

"Gino did WHAT?!" I could hear Mother yelling, and the house seemed to rattle as she pounded her way down the stairs and thundered into the doorway.

"What did you do?" she asked me. "Did you put cleanser in Rachel's teacup?!"

Perhaps I was emboldened by my relationship with Shippy and Jennifer, but this was a bald-faced lie. For the first time, I stood up for myself.

"No, I did not! SHE put it in MY teacup! I spit it out, and it hit her. It was an accident!"

Mother looked confused now. She wasn't used to us talking back. She shoved past me and knocked me over as she attempted to get to the scene of the crime. Seeing how the tea party was laid out and where the spit had landed, she turned her back on us.

"Who was sitting in the tub?" No one said a word. "I know someone was sitting in the tub! Who was it?"

Michael slowly raised his hand, pointed directly at Rachel Jr., and said "her" in a voice so small, it would have been inaudible if the room had not been in absolute silence. I was shocked! I could not believe Michael had come to my rescue. Rachel couldn't believe it either. The facts were incontrovertible. Her smug grimace faded as Mother turned on her.

"Rachel, were you sitting in this tub?"

Rachel Jr.'s jaw slackened, and she could barely croak out the words "Yes, Mamma."

"Boys, go upstairs," Mother ordered. She didn't need to tell us twice. We were down the hall and halfway up the stairs before she finished her sentence.

When Mother reappeared upstairs twenty minutes later, she was puffing and red in the face.

"Boys, go wash up for dinner. Rachel won't be joining us."

Pa had arrived home, and the four of us sat down to eat. Very little was said.

When dinner was over, Michael and I helped with the dishes and then sat down to do our homework. Mother allowed us to watch some TV and then sent us both off to bed.

The next morning, all hell broke loose.

Pa went through his usual routine of getting us all out of bed. As he headed down the hall to get Rachel Jr. out of bed, I heard him say, "What on Earth is that smell," and then, "Oh my God!" as he walked into the bathroom. Michael and I were still rubbing our eyes as Pa went back into Rachel Jr.'s room and called Mother to come down using the intercom.

Mother was downstairs in a flash and stormed down the hall with Pa. I heard her gasp as she entered the bathroom.

"That's it, Richard! He's out of here! You know what this kind of thing means as well as I do!" Mother gathered up Rachel Jr. and Michael and whisked them away from me as if I were a leper. I was still sitting on my bed. Without even realizing it, I had assumed my standard position—feet dangling from the side of the bed, hands folded in my lap, and head hung low. I'm sure I looked guilty, but I had no idea what I was guilty of.

Pa appeared moments after Mother had dragged Rachel Jr. and Michael upstairs.

"Gino," he said in a calm and very level tone as if speaking to a crazy person, "please come with me."

Without looking up I slid off the bed and followed him down the hall. As we got closer to the bathroom, I began to smell something very foul. By the time we reached the bathroom door, the smell was so intense I thought I would vomit. Pa flicked on the light and handed me a rag and a bucket.

"You need to clean this up. I'll be waiting for you in the bedroom."

He walked out and closed the door behind him. I stood in the bathroom, still in my pajamas, with a huge bucket in one hand and a rag in the other looking at a sight I will never forget. Human feces had been smeared over the entire bathroom. It was on the walls, in the sink, in the bathtub, all over the toilet, and even on the back of the door. Once I realized what I was expected to clean up, I dropped the bucket and the rag and ran back to my room.

"I didn't do it! Why do you think I did it?"

Pa didn't say a word. He stood, picked me up, and carried me back down the hall to the bathroom. Once inside the bathroom, he put me down, turned around, and walked out, shutting the door behind him once more. I didn't care how much Mother would beat me, I wasn't cleaning this up. The smell was overpowering. I yanked at the door, but it wouldn't open. Pa was on the other side holding it shut. I pulled and pulled, but it did no good. Feeling panic rising from deep inside of me, I started to scream for someone to let me out and hurled the entire weight of my body at the door.

"Gino, you have to clean up that mess before you can come out. I don't care how long you scream or cry, you're not coming out until it's clean." Pa had the same calm and level tone in his voice as he had when I first met him.

I had no choice. When I had pulled myself together, I started at the task. Ten minutes in, I began to vomit. The vomiting turned to uncontrollable dry heaving. I couldn't breathe. At this point, Pa's righteousness must have been overcome by his conscience. He opened the door and told me to get up and go back to my room. I ran down the hall, sobbing, and threw myself onto my bed. I grabbed hold of Sparky and rocked myself back and forth. As Pa walked past, he told me I was to stay in my room until he came down to get me.

I was still in my pajamas when Jay arrived. She came down to my room and sat on my bed. I started sobbing again. I had done nothing wrong, but I felt a tremendous sense of guilt and remorse. Jay put her arms around me and didn't say a word. She just let me cry. When I had cried as much as I was going to, she told me I would be leaving the following morning. All I could say was that I didn't do it, which I kept repeating over and over. Jay told me not to worry about it. Everything was going to be okay.

She picked me up the following morning. I never got to say goodbye to Shippy and Jennifer, but I was glad to be free from Mother and Rachel Jr. I also never found out for sure who spread their feces all over the bathroom, but it wasn't me, and I doubt very much it was Michael.

But what now? If people like Mother and Pa didn't want me, then no one would. There had been so much loss and disappointment in my life so far, that I was resigned to the fact I would never have a family or a place to call home. I had given up hope.

As an adult, I have come to understand that the word of foster parents is considered unquestionable, and reports of a foster child's mental health are entered into that child's permanent record. Smearing one's own feces is considered one of the most severe signs of emotional instability in a child.

Somewhere in Sonoma County, there is a file that says that's what I did. It exists because Mother found it easier to blame a temporary foster kid than to admit her daughter might have had mental illness or question her own skills as a parent. This is another way abusive foster parents can create indelible marks on the psyches of children—by telling falsehoods that become matters of record and literally rewriting someone's personal history.

CHAPTER 8

Falling Through the Cracks

When Jay came to pick me up from Camp Meeker, she told me they were still working on the paperwork to get me back into the Dependent Unit, so I was to stay in the 601 Unit for a couple of weeks. They were still trying to get me back into the system after the failed adoption attempt with the Nielsons and had nowhere else to put me, especially now that I was on record as having signs of "severe psychological damage."

The 601 Unit was located within the Sonoma County Juvenile Hall. It was where runaways were taken after being picked up by the police. They were given the choice of calling their parents and going home or returning to the streets. They had forty-eight hours to make their choice. If they chose to return to the streets and were picked up again, they were pipelined to juvenile hall.

When we arrived at the unit, I was afraid of all of the bars and barbed wire. It looked like what it was—a prison. We entered the common room, which was the size of a large family room and featured an old sofa and a cabinet-style TV. Opposite the TV was an in-line industrial kitchen. The room was presided over by a large woman in a grayish corrections uniform crowded behind an undersized beige desk of faux wood. Opposite the woman at the desk was a long hallway with twelve cells, six on each side. The cell doors were solid steel with no openings save a small, barred window at the top.

As Jay talked with the woman at the desk, I explored the cells. Each cell had a small steel-framed bed, a sink, and a toilet. Other than the window at the top of the door, each also had a tiny, barred window to the yard—its sole communication with the outside world.

When my social worker and the lady at the desk were finished talking, they came over to me, and the woman pointed to the first cell on the right and told me that would be my "room."

Jay reassured me this was temporary and said she would be back again soon. As soon as she was gone, I went into my "room" to get something, and the steel door slammed shut with a deafening bang. I started screaming as loud as I could but got no response. In panicked desperation, I started throwing my body against my cell door as I had done in the bathroom in Camp Meeker.

"What's going on in there? For God's sake, don't hurt yourself!"

The woman came puffing up the hall jangling her keys. As soon as she reopened the door, I flew past her, sprinting as fast as I could to the driveway. Jay was just pulling away, and when she saw me running and screaming toward her, she stopped and got out of the car. I begged her not to leave me there.

"I promise that whatever it was I did to deserve being put in jail I won't do it again! I don't want to be locked up."

She looked down at me with a puzzled expression.

"Locked up? You're not here to be locked up."

I told her the woman at the desk had locked me in right after she left. Jay stormed back inside with me. Her second conversation with the woman at the desk was nowhere near as friendly as the first had been. The policy for when runaway kids came into the unit was that they be locked in their cells for the first twenty-four hours—no exceptions. After the initial twenty-four-hour period, they were allowed to stay for one more day and think about what they wanted to do. The role of the woman behind the desk was purely administrative. She was not to interact with the runaways.

Jay informed her in no uncertain terms I was not a runaway and the rules did not apply to me. If there was another incident, supervisors would be notified. Once the woman behind the desk realized her mistake, she apologized to me and assured me it wouldn't happen again. After a while, I was able to calm down and Jay was reassured enough to leave again. I lay down on the couch, too afraid of being locked up to go to my room.

That evening, there was a shift change and another woman was sitting at the desk when I woke up. The new woman was much kinder and even got me to go to my cell for the night. Of all the women that sat at the desk during a twenty-four-hour period, the nighttime woman quickly became my favorite.

It took about a week for me to adjust to my new surroundings. Once I got used to it, it seemed like a pretty good gig. I didn't have to go to school and got to watch TV all day if I wanted. At the beginning of each day, an older man came to deliver whatever food I had ordered the previous day. The food was delivered unprepared, so I had to cook it. Whatever woman was behind the desk at the time was prohibited by policy from physically helping me but would talk me through the process of preparing my meals from her desk. I would pull out my little stepstool, stand at the stove, and follow the instructions being given by the woman behind the desk. This was how I learned to cook at eight years old.

Teenage runaways came and went, so I wasn't often alone. A kid would come in, get locked in their cell for twenty-four hours, and then leave. Sadly, most of the kids that came through the 601 Unit during my stay there chose to return to the streets. Once in a while, there would be some crying, but the process was generally uneventful. One afternoon, a pretty, young girl of about sixteen came in. She was processed by the woman at the desk and then marched down the hall and locked in her cell, where she began to sob piteously. I knew the policy. She was going to be in there for a while, so I got a chair and dragged it down the hall to her cell door.

She must have been surprised to see a little kid peering in her window, but when we started talking, she began to calm down. She told me her home life was awful and all she did was fight with her mom, who was too strict. She begged me to let her out of her cell, and I said I'd see what I could do.

It took me half of that day to soften up the woman behind the desk, but by now, I knew how to charm her. It took some doing, but in time she relented and let the girl out. The girl and I sat on the couch and talked all afternoon. She spoke of her life as I sat and listened. I think the reason she sticks out in my memory so much is because, to me, she had what seemed like a great life. She had two parents that loved her, and her biggest complaint was that she couldn't get along with her mother.

My irritation with her grew until I could no longer hide it. When she asked me what was wrong, I said, "I would be happy to have just one parent that loved me."

I'll never forget the look on her face. She said nothing but got up and asked the woman behind the desk to use the phone. She called her parents, and they were there within half an hour. When her mother asked what made her decide to come home, she pointed at me and said, "That little guy." Her parents hugged me and the three of them left together. They did come back one other time and brought me some toys, including a stuffed teddy bear I named Barney, but I never saw them again after that.

I was in the 601 Unit for four months, which is an eternity to an eight-year-old. I never thought I'd miss school, but I did. There was a constant stream of runaways, so I wasn't alone often, but when I was, I would watch TV and act out being a pirate. Playing pirate was one of my favorite things to do. I didn't have any toys other than a few stuffed animals, so I had to make do with what I had. Using Kleenex around my wrists and neck to imitate a pirate shirt, I'd "air sword" fight around the common room for the entertainment of the woman behind the desk. Sometimes I would make my sole purpose of the day to make her laugh. I wouldn't say we became friends, but I think we developed an understanding.

Despite all that had come before, I still consider those few months in the 601 Unit as the lowest point in my childhood. It not only marked my return to the system but starting over again from the very bottom—institutionalized and alone. Other than the parade of temporary runaways, it was a period of solitary confinement brought about for no reason other than a muddle of paperwork. I think this sort of slipup has been largely eradicated today. Since my time in the system, there have been many caring people working hard to close these types of cracks in the system so kids don't slip through. That doesn't mean it never happens, though.

After a few months, my paperwork went through to return me to the Dependent Unit. I said goodbye to the lady behind the desk, and Jay drove me down the road for what was to be my third and final stay.

CHAPTER 9

Don't Give Up Hope

Of my three stays at the Dependent Unit, this is the one that remains clearest in my memory. I was nearly nine by the time I arrived. In addition to being my last experience there, it was also the longest. I was there for almost a full year by the time a home was found for me.

The building was less than a quarter of a mile down the road from the 601 Unit. By now I was quite familiar with being processed in. Everything I owned—stuffed animals and a few pieces of old clothing—was still carried in a large black garbage bag. I couldn't have cared less about the clothes, but the stuffed animals were my "friends." Other than the time I was at the Children's Garden, I had never been in one place long enough to make friends. My stuffed animals, however, were always with me.

I recognized a few of the staff from my last stay and waved to them as I was guided through the halls. My room was the last room on the right in the boy's hall. I shared it with one other boy, a strapping twelve-year-old named Aaron. His hair was the same shade of blond as mine and our eye color was identical, but he stood about five feet ten inches and had a muscular frame, making me look like the smaller version of him. Aaron was a very masculine boy, and the girls in the Dependent Unit fawned over him. I was petrified of him at first, but I soon came to regard him with great admiration.

He, however, had little time for an effeminate nine-year-old. He ignored me and barely spoke to me at first, but over the next few weeks, I was able to build a kinship and, in time, something like little-brother status.

For the first few months, I followed Aaron around everywhere. He was the coolest kid there and he took good care of me. Then things changed. A girl came in and stole Aaron away from me. She was a very pretty Hispanic girl named Maria. At sixteen, she was the oldest of the girls, and Aaron was just twelve, but Maria didn't care. She put her sights on him, and I went from the cool little brother to the pain-in-the-ass little brother overnight. Aaron did his best to shake me, but he soon figured out it was impossible to scare me away.

Before long, Maria had Aaron wrapped around her little finger and he would do just about anything for her. Aaron was a typical preteen boy going through puberty, and Maria gave him just what he wanted: sex, and lots of it, which didn't do much to ingratiate her much with me.

Obviously, sex between kids in the Unit was strictly forbidden, but Aaron and Maria were wily beyond their years. As I was ever eager to please and always at Aaron's heels, it didn't take him long to find a use for me. I became their lookout and greatest ally to their exploits. I stood guard for them many, many times or played the decoy to distract the staff. It didn't matter where we were. They would go at it and were done in a flash (he was only twelve, after all).

It wasn't long before Aaron and Maria became the Dependent Unit's version of a "power couple." As the oldest girl, she was soon seen as a surrogate mother to all of the kids. As her "man," Aaron became the father. Some of the younger children even started referring to them as Mom and Dad, at least when there were no staff members in sight.

Of course, it couldn't go on forever. When the day came and they were caught, both were put on X step, but even that did little to stop them.

The steps were basically letter grades we earned based on our behavior. Higher grades, such as A or B step, meant more privileges. Lower grades, including the lowest dreaded X step, meant having privileges stripped away.

Anyone on X step had their bed hauled into one of the game rooms with a wall of windows looking out onto the main living area so everyone could see. Once a kid reached the top of the scale, they could earn bonus points. The points could then be exchanged for toys or candy from the "points closet" at the end of the week. This system was meant to both reinforce good behavior and teach us the rudiments of financial management without having to use money.

The most common reason kids were placed on X step was attempting to run away, which was a frequent occurrence. Just outside of the room I shared with Aaron was an emergency exit door to the outside. The older kids used this door to escape. They never got very far. The second the alarm went off, the police were called. When the kids that had attempted to run away were brought back, they ended up on X step.

When Aaron and Maria were placed on X step for their sexual exploits, Aaron had to move to the common room. I was alone once more. I often lay awake at night in terror, clutching one of my stuffed animals. I had come to think of Aaron as my protector. When he returned, I was thrilled to see him again, but my happiness was short-lived.

One night at about 2 a.m., I heard the emergency exit alarm, and before I even looked up, I knew it was Aaron. At almost the same moment I heard the alarm in the girls' hall go off, and I knew it was Maria. I jumped out of bed and scurried to the open door. There was a full moon that night, and the brightness of the moon lit up the cow pastures surrounding the Dependent Unit as if it were daytime. Like something out of a cheesy romance movie, Maria and Aaron ran toward each other and embraced before running off into the darkness. At age nine, I thought it was incredibly romantic, although even then, I realized how stupid and futile it was.

A few days later Aaron and Maria were both back and on X step again. This was not the first time either had run away, but it was the first time they had run away together. Within hours after the two had returned, I was informed I would be moving into a single-occupant room across the hall from the one I had been sharing with Aaron.

Up until this point in my life, I had always done what I was told and gone peacefully wherever the representatives of the system sent me. I had such low self-esteem that I didn't think I had the right to stand up for myself. I felt lucky that anyone would take me, so I never complained. But for some reason, the news of being forced to move out of my room for someone else's stupid behavior was the final straw that sent me over the edge. Maybe I was mad Maria had succeeded in stealing my only friend from me. It's hard to know why some things triggered my rage while other, more horrific things left me numb. The things that triggered me, however, drove me into a rage in an instant. I think it's safe to say I had developed significant PTSD by this point.

During my time at Children's Garden, I had learned how to channel my anger in healthier ways. I was taught that running around, screaming into my pillow, or sometimes just walking away were all healthy ways to express my anger. But in that moment, it all disappeared. I yelled and screamed at the staff, called them all assholes, and stormed off in a huff. Even as I was doing it, I could visualize my name sliding down the step chart. I didn't care. I stomped outside in a rage and just kept walking. I got all the way down the long drive to a massive stump and sat there for about half an hour.

When I had calmed myself down enough to make peace with the change of rooms, I walked up the drive and back into the building. My name had been moved to X step on the big board as a "runaway." This had to be a mistake. I ran down the boy's hall to what was supposed to be my new room, but it was empty. Hoping they had changed their minds and left me in my old room, I checked there next. It, too, was empty. With my head hung low, I shuffled up to the counter in the main hall and was told to go to my room. The counselor was pointing at the game room. I did as I was instructed, sat on my bed, and sobbed.

This being my first offense, I didn't spend too much time on X step. I moved back into the boy's hall and into my single room. I decided it wasn't so bad once I got used to it. At least I didn't have to listen to Aaron's snoring.

Maria ended up pregnant with Aaron's baby. Then she just disappeared one day. Aaron succeeded in running away not long after, or else he was caught and put in a different facility. I never saw him again.

About two or three weeks after my "attempted running away," things started to look up a bit and I found a new friend. A new kid I had known for a short time at Children's Garden arrived at the Dependent Unit. Tommy had moved into the house with the older couple about two weeks before I left, so I didn't know him very well. I had only a vague memory of him, but the moment he saw me he came right up to me, and we formed a quick bond. The distraction Tommy provided was healthy for me, as it pulled me away from the perpetual cloud of drama that surrounded Aaron and Maria.

Tommy was a year older than I was and was bigger. He was a nice kid, but something wasn't right about him. He was very rough and forceful with me. He seemed to take pleasure in pinning me down and making me do things I didn't want to do. Sometimes he would try to get me to experiment with him sexually. I wasn't interested, but he managed to convince me once. I relented just to shut him up. He tried to have anal sex with me, telling me it wouldn't hurt, but of course it did, so I shoved him off and put a stop to his advances by telling on him. He got in trouble, and we didn't talk much for a while.

Other than the sex stuff and borderline bullying, I enjoyed having a buddy my age. Beggars can't be choosers. But, as tended to happen with friends in the system, Tommy was sent away. I have no idea where he was taken, and I never saw him again.

Of course, not all my experiences at the Dependent Unit were difficult. Once again, there was a sense of stability and continuity to life. There were also occasional moments of outright joy. I remember one school bus driver who got along well with all the kids. I was old enough to be going to public school by this time, and the ride to and from the Dependent Unit's remote location took some time. The driver came up with a genius plan to keep us all occupied and well-behaved. The most popular song at the time was Diana Ross's "Upside Down." The bus driver played it every day and assigned parts based on where we sat on the bus. By the end of the school year, we knew it so well, she had created a little dance routine to go along with it.

The ride home from school became my favorite part of the day as the yellow diesel bus chugged past golden fields of befuddled cows with a full load of kids waving and wiggling in unison while chirping along to the iconic disco melody at the top of our lungs.

It wasn't long after Tommy left that I was assigned a new social worker, and she turned out to be the best one I ever had. To this day I am grateful to her for her hard work and the dedication she showed on my behalf.

Kathee spoke with a soft, nurturing voice, and I was transfixed by her beauty. I remember shaking her hand and being struck by its softness. She had long, curly brown hair that fell to the side of her face, showing off her high cheekbones and flawless skin. I knew from the start she was safe and trustworthy. My internal security system of red flags, bells, and whistles was silent and calm whenever she was near.

Kathee and I sat in a large conference room off the administrative area of the Dependent Unit and talked for what seemed like hours. She was one of the first people I had ever met that sat and spoke *with* me instead of *at* me. Her interest in me seemed genuine and honest, and, somehow, I knew meeting her was a huge step forward on my journey.

As I sat and got to know Kathee, she gave me some paper and crayons and asked me to draw her some pictures—a distraction method to get me to relax as we talked. She told me she worked for a private foundation known as the Casey Family Program. At the time, this meant nothing to me, but now I am able to look back and see that becoming a part of this organization is most likely what saved my life. It also marked my transition from short-term to long-term care, which is what the Casey Family Program specialized in. I often wonder what would have happened to me if I had stayed in the care of the county foster system.

I can't remember if it was during our initial visit or soon thereafter, but at some point, Kathee told me she had found a family that would like to meet me. I had been through this before, so I knew what kind of outward reaction was expected. I did my best to act excited and hopeful. Inside, I felt nothing but indifference. By this time, I knew better than to hope. But sometimes life hands you a gift when you least expect it. The family Kathee had found for me would be one of the greatest gifts of my life. It was the beginning of a path toward healing—a path that would have many ups and downs, but began with a small flicker of hope.

The Casey Family Program (now known as Casey Family Programs) is a community-centered nonprofit. Throughout my childhood, it was instrumental in helping me overcome trauma, build hope, and provide the skills to allow me to become successful as an adult. The organization was started by James E. Casey, the founder of UPS, back in 1966, to support vulnerable children. It is now a nationwide program, but when I entered it, they had just started expanding from Washington state. I was one of the first batch of kids in California to be adopted into the program. CFP still operates today and now impacts and improves the lives of countless kids. You can find out more about them at casey.org.

I had one more experience at the Dependent Unit as an adult. I was working for an insurance company, and we were brainstorming a charity idea for the Christmas holiday. Looking back on my experiences at the Dependent Unit, I suggested a "Toys for Tots" type drive to benefit the kids that were there. The team loved it. I called the Unit and was sent a wish list with every kid that was housed there and what they wanted. My co-workers were thrilled and went all out, buying everything on the list and then some. When we had all the presents, I went with my boyfriend at the time to drop them off.

The staff there aren't supposed to let any adults into the area where the children live, but hearing I was there several times during my youth, they allowed me to have a look around and even see my old room. It was a powerful experience that brought me to tears, but one thing I noticed is that it looked much more inviting than when I was there as a child. Gone were the metallic beds with synthetic institutional spreads. Instead, each had a unique quilt. The lady giving us the tour told me the quilts were from a circle of local women who donated them so each child could have something they knew was their own. When the kids left, they took the quilts with them. She then turned to me.

"Didn't you get a quilt?"

"No," I said. "They must have started after I was here."

"Well, come on then." She led me to the office where I had been processed in so many years before and opened up a huge closet door. Inside were stacks of neatly folded quilts. "Pick one."

My eyes were so full of tears, I could barely see to choose. In the end, we left with two. I still have them as a reminder that things are getting better and there will always be people who care enough to do the little things that make a big difference.

CHAPTER 10

The Price of Unconditional Love

The day I was to meet my new prospective parents, Kathee came to pick me up. I was much more excited to see her than I was to meet them, as I had developed a bit of a crush on her. As we drove, she told me a little about the couple I was going to meet.

They lived in Fairfax, a small town in Marin County, but had immigrated from Germany. When I asked if they had any other kids, Kathee became noticeably uncomfortable.

"They *did*, yes. Their son got very sick a couple of years ago and died."

I wasn't sure how to respond, so I just said, "Oh…wow! That's really sad."

The drive took us a bit out of town and into a nature park. As Kathee's car crunched across the gravel lot, I saw them standing near a fence. Helmut was a tall, slender man with slicked gray hair. His face was stern but softened when he saw me. His eyes were steel blue and he stood with his hands behind his back. Bruni was short and stocky, but not fat. Her dark curls were lifted off her neck in a style from yesteryear. Her eyes twinkled and she looked jolly. When she spoke, it was with a thick German accent. Her face told me all I needed to know—she wanted me. I knew right away Helmut was going to take more convincing. Even though my instincts told me he was kind, he seemed sad and guarded. I took his hand as we were introduced and did something I had never done before while meeting adoptive parents; I took him on a short walk away from Kathee and Bruni and spoke with him directly.

My appeal must have worked because the couple invited me for a day visit not long after. Kathee picked me up from the Dependent Unit and drove me all the way to the couple's house in the Fairfax hills. When we pulled in front of the main gate, my jaw dropped. I had heard Helmut had made the massive wrought iron gate himself. It made their home seem like a castle to me.

Kathee honked her horn and Helmut came striding up the driveway, hands behind his back, and let us in. By the time we reached the house, Bruni was standing in front of the garage smiling from ear to ear. I jumped out of the car, gave them both a big hug, and we went into what would soon be my new home.

We entered the house through a side door (they never used the front entrance) that opened into a wood-paneled TV room. This seemed nothing short of palatial to me. What kind of mansion had a whole other room besides the living room just for TV?

I was still taking it in when someone asked me if I wanted to go swimming.

"Swim?" I asked. "Swim where?"

"There," said Helmut, pointing out the window to a wooded area in the backyard. "We have a pool on our property."

I squirmed with excitement. "YES! I love to swim!"

As Bruni took me to get a suit, we walked through the main living room. I was in awe. I had never seen anything like it. The ceiling seemed a hundred feet high and there was a wall of windows overlooking the valley below. In front of the windows sat a grand-looking dining table and a huge half-circle sofa that matched the valances running along the top of the wall of windows. The fireplace looked big enough for me to stand up inside it. Just to the right of it, a large piano gleamed. I learned later that Bruni had a hobby of making stained glass. One large piece depicting a hummingbird and colorful flowers hung in the central window, casting amber and crimson rays on the floor. I felt like I was dreaming, like someone must have made a mistake.

There was also a picture of a little boy on one wall that looked very much like me at age two. This was Freddy. He was almost exactly my age when he died and looked like he could have been my twin. I wasn't a replacement for what they had lost, exactly, but at least for Bruni, I was someone to love and care for. The arrangement might seem macabre in retrospect, and it was not without its problems; the image of a child I never knew but always felt compared to literally hung over me. But I didn't see that at the time, just a glimmer of hope.

Bruni opened the door to my room and I got a glimpse of it. It was almost more than I could take. There were windows everywhere. To a kid who lived in a cell not long ago, this was shocking, to say the least. One wall was covered with beautiful wood shelves full of all kinds of toys and cool kid stuff, each more enticing than the last. A desk that matched the shelves faced the window and a sloping view to the wooded property beyond. The full-size bed seemed enormous to me. I knew I shouldn't get too excited because Bruni and Helmut would undoubtedly change their minds. No one who lived this way could possibly want me.

Bruni had prepared for my visit by buying me a pair of swim trunks. I was changed in a flash and tried not to hop up and down in my excitement over the pool. The water was freezing cold, but I didn't care. It was summertime, and the weather was warm. I swam for the whole visit. I couldn't believe this was happening to me. I figured I might as well take advantage before they changed their minds.

The next step in the process was regular weekend visits. I remember these seemed to go on for months—much longer than they had before with other families. Bruni would come every Friday and pick me up. We almost always stopped and bought cheese at the Sonoma Cheese Factory on our way home. On Sunday, both Bruni and Helmut would take me back to the Dependent Unit. I always hated going back. I was sure each time would be the last time I'd see them, that they'd wise up and realize I didn't deserve them as a family.

But then one Friday afternoon, Bruni came to pick me up and I left the Dependent Unit for good. My life changed forever. By now I had been there for almost a full year, which was longer than most kids ever stayed. I was happy to leave and never looked back.

Life with Bruni and Helmut was wonderful for me. Bruni and I formed an instant and unbreakable bond. She loved me so much that even when she got angry at me, I could tell it would pass. I wasn't used to that kind of love. Until Bruni entered my life, I had been completely unaware of the concept of unconditional love. In my mind, there were always costs to be weighed and performances to put on. I could never just be me and be loved. I always had to fill the role others expected of me. With Bruni it was different. I grew to know that no matter how difficult I became, she would never willingly abandon me. She was my savior when I needed one the most. I can never express how much I love her and appreciate all she has done for me. She showed me adults could be trusted.

Although I knew Helmut loved me too, my relationship with him was quite different. Both he and Bruni had grown up in Germany during World War Two, but where Bruni had come out of that trauma with a nurturing need to be kind and gentle, Helmut was gruff, firm, and sometimes distant. There were times when his soft side came through, but he and I often quarreled. Bruni loved me wildly and without reservation for who I was, but with Helmut, I always sensed I came up lacking. The weight of comparison with the perfect child they had lost was always in the background. It was even more apparent when my behavioral problems crept back in through the safety of their world.

Regardless of how they felt about me, it was crystal clear to me they adored each other. Through their love, support, and the stability they offered, I began to see that there might be hope for me after all—that I might be worthy of being loved.

Christmas 1980 was the most magical Christmas of my life. By that time, I was ten and considered myself a worldly big kid. I scoffed at those who still believed in things like Santa Claus. I knew with absolute certainty that there was no such thing.

That changed when we returned from a holiday party at a neighbor's house across the road on Christmas Eve. As we arrived home, coming in through the side door as always, Bruni peeled me out of my layers of clothes and told me to go put my pajamas on. As I opened the door from the kitchen to the main living room, I stepped into a dream.

The enormous Christmas tree stretched up to the vaulted ceiling. It was ablaze with a galaxy of twinkling white lights. Beneath it, a sea of presents spilled out across the living room floor. There were so many I didn't even know where to start. I looked back into the kitchen at Helmut and Bruni. They were acting as if nothing was going on.

"Bruni! Bruni!" I shouted. "Did you see this?"

She looked up from her perch at the kitchen sink and said, "What are you talking about?" Then she started to walk toward the door to the living room with Helmut right behind her. The look of genuine surprise on their faces convinced me they had nothing to do with the transformation of our living room.

"Well, I guess Santa is very busy this year because he came early," Helmut said in the tone one might employ to state that water was wet. My steadfast belief that Santa did not exist evaporated. There simply was no other explanation for what I was looking at. It was my Christmas miracle.

There were more presents than I could have imagined. A stereo system, a brand-new twelve-speed bicycle, the biggest teddy bear I had ever seen, a remote-controlled motorboat for the pool, and countless other gifts, each fantastical and carefully selected. It seemed to take all night to get through the presents Santa had brought for me despite being in a frenzy and tearing through them at lighting speed. Helmut and Bruni laughed at my delight and chased me around trying to catch the flying wrapping paper. They seemed happier that night than I had ever seen them. Helmut was smiling from ear to ear and Bruni's eyes were filled with warmth and love. For the first time

I could remember, I felt like the luckiest little boy in the world. It was the family I had always dreamed of.

The next two years were full of ups and downs. I spent most of the summers in the pool. One of my favorite adventures was turning on all the sprinklers and scooting around the pool on an inflatable boat using the hose as a propulsion system. I would pretend to be a great adventurer deep in the rainforest. Of course, Helmut put a stop to quite so much adventuring when the water bill came due and the area around the pool turned into a swamp.

As I began to feel safer, however, I also began to feel less worthy of all that Helmut and Bruni were doing for me. Private school, piano lessons, pool parties—all experiences that were so far from the life I had known up to this point that I couldn't process them. At the same time, the shadow of Freddy was always in the background. I had the same piano teacher and even wore many of the same clothes before I outgrew them.

It is not uncommon for children who have suffered abuse early in their development to have feelings of low self-worth. When they find a healthy, caring, and supportive relationship, whether with parents, romantic partners, or friends, the new relationship clashes with their own view of themselves as worthless. It seems too good to be true.

No matter how safe and loving Bruni and Helmut were, there was always a part of me that thought *this will never last. Eventually they will see me for who I am and find me unworthy of their love.* I began to test the relationship. Certain of eventual abandonment and desperate not to become attached before it happened, I began acting out again, intentionally making life difficult for the very people who supported me.

Creeping into this mix of emotions was the growing unconscious fear that I would never measure up to the memory of Freddy. There was always the question of whether they loved me for me, or just as a second-rate substitute for the golden child they would never get back.

The more Bruni accepted my ensuing disrespect, the more convinced I was that I was unworthy of her love. Thus, the cycle continued.

I fought her—especially her—tooth and nail. Just getting me out of bed for school became a herculean battle. No matter how much of a brat I acted like, Bruni's love never wavered, not even for a second. She still tucked me in at night and greeted me kindly every morning when I would get out of bed. When I was sure this would be the day they had given up, my breakfast would be waiting for me at the table. Some mornings I was so filled with shame I didn't even want to eat.

Psychologists call this "obsessive defiance disorder." It takes a very delicate balance of reassurance, love, and healthy structure to counter this spiral, and some never get over it. As much as Bruni loved me unconditionally, this was also her handicap. She loved without boundaries.

I remember one incident where I was supposed to take a bath. For a kid who loved the pool so much, I hated bath time. I was determined to have my toys if I was going to take a bath and was throwing a fit like a toddler. I knew they were in a high cupboard, so I went over and yanked a chair to stand on. I didn't realize as I did so that Bruni was just about to sit down. She landed hard on the floor and started screaming in pain. I thought I had killed her, but she had just broken her tailbone. She had to drive sitting on a pillow for weeks afterward. I felt terrible. It took her until I was about thirty-five to believe I hadn't done it on purpose, but she never let me live it down.

When we reminisced on those years later in life, she would sigh and say, "You ver a challengink child." She taught me every day is another chance to start over.

After the first year or so, Helmut's job started to require him to fly to San Luis Obispo every Monday morning. Bruni would take him to a private airfield in Oakland, and then she and I would drive out to pick him up on Thursday evening. This left Bruni and me alone much of the time. I did not make it easy for her. She had to fight me on everything. I was old enough to know I was being unfair to her and was filled with intense guilt but couldn't stop myself. Kathee came to our house several times a week to work with our family. I had never seen so much of a social worker in my life. This went on for the next year or two. As much as Bruni still loved me, what I didn't see was how it was affecting Helmut. He could see what was happening and had his own concerns.

Even when Bruni yelled at me, I just laughed because of her thick accent. The only time I remember her showing even the slightest hint of physical aggression was when I was doing something I shouldn't have while she was out working in the yard. She got furious and told me to cut it out. I yelled back at her, and she turned the hose on me. This incident sticks out in my mind even among all the instances of physical abuse by others because I was so shocked by how out of character it was. She must have been at her wits' end with me that day.

Aside from school and normal family activities, Bruni and Helmut were sure to take me to events put on by the Casey Family Program so I could interact with other foster kids like me. It was at one of these events, an annual picnic the year I turned eleven, that I met Anne Mirci and her adopted daughters, Claudia and Maria. Claudia and Maria were biological half sisters and were also Casey kids about my age. We played and got along well together at the picnic, as Anne befriended Helmut and Bruni.

Claudia was a slender, pretty girl of Hispanic and African American descent. She was a year older than I was, and we developed a bit of a crush on one another. Maria was a short, stout, Hispanic girl with a Mary Lou Retton haircut. She was two years older than me. The girls shared the same birth mother but different fathers.

Anne was a respected teacher in the Livermore school system. She had wavy, shoulder-length hair and a slight Southern twang. She was just over fifty when I met her and had a penchant for tight polyester pants that did little for her heavy frame. She also wore large glasses popular in the era with transitional lenses that darkened in the sunlight to shade her pale blue eyes.

A few weeks after our first meeting, during one of her many visits, Kathee asked me if I would like to spend the weekend with Anne and the girls in Livermore. I was thrilled and jumped at the opportunity. I had so much fun with Anne and the girls that when it came time for me to leave, I didn't want to go home. I went back a few more times over the course of the next year and always had a wonderful time. They seemed like the perfect family.

On a cold and rainy afternoon in the fall of 1982—just as I was starting the sixth grade at my small private school—I came home, and everything had changed. Kathee was there, which wasn't unusual given my constant behavior problems, but this time I hadn't known she was coming. Nobody had told me. The alarm bells and whistles I had long thought silent were going off in my head with such intensity I felt I was going to explode.

I was in the small TV room with a friend, and when he left, Kathee, Helmut, and Bruni came into the room. I knew by the look on their faces that it was over. I was going to be leaving for good.

Bruni had tears in her eyes as I was given the news. This time something was different, though. In the past, I had been told I was leaving or just taken away to wherever they could find a place to put me. Now, Kathee *asked* if I would like to go to live with Anne and the girls. I cannot recall the reason given, but I do remember no one ever said it was my fault. In fact, I believe Kathee made a point of telling me it *wasn't* my fault. I had never seen Helmut show sadness before, but as Kathee delivered the news I would be moving again, he too had tears in his eyes and had to leave the room.

I didn't find out why I had been removed from Helmut and Bruni's care until I was an adult. Helmut had been diagnosed with terminal colon cancer and he, knowing how difficult I was with Bruni, felt I would be too much for her to handle alone, particularly while dealing with the grief of losing a husband. Unfortunately, it meant that in addition to losing her husband, she was forced to come to terms with losing me too. After the loss of their first boy, it must have been a devastating decision to make.

Several months after I left, Bruni called me to give me the news that Helmut had passed away. I can remember feeling overwhelmed by guilt. I felt as if I had killed him by being such a terrible child, and now Bruni was alone. At the time, I had no idea he had even been sick and was crushed at not being able to say goodbye to him.

Bruni stayed in my life for the rest of hers. I never called her my grandmother to her face, but that's how I came to think of her. She remained an integral part of my life through adulthood. She even made me a birthday cake every year until her death in 2018. I now believe that part of the reason we remained so close is because, at the very core of who we are, we understood one another through our shared experience of loss. She was never the same as when I first met her. A part of her died with Helmut.

The day I moved from Helmut and Bruni's care to Anne's care was a day that will always be imprinted on my memory. At the time I had no way of knowing my life was about to take a sharp turn. The next three years brought so much torment that without the foundation of hope and self-worth Helmut and Bruni had given me, I do not think I would have survived it.

A few years after I married Tony and we were in the middle of building our house, I asked Bruni if she had any stained-glass pieces in storage that I could have as decorations. She insisted on giving me the hummingbird piece that had hung in the living room window the entire time I lived with her and Helmut. At first, I couldn't take it. It was, after all, her favorite. But she continued to insist. Tony said we could have a door custom-made to fit the glass so we would always be reminded of her. This is now the door to the kitchen from the laundry room, and I think of her every time I pass by it.

As kind as she was to me, Bruni always had harsh things to say about Kathee. I later learned this was because, upon realizing she could no longer care for me, Bruni struggled to find me a home with my biological family. She couldn't understand why the foster care system couldn't divulge information about them. She often took this frustration out on Kathee as the representative of the system. I am forever grateful Bruni got to see me united with my loving biological family before she passed away.

Of course, her efforts at reuniting me with them took place well before the days of the internet. Now, social workers do everything they can to unite kids with their biological families, if at all possible, and probably couldn't keep that information concealed even if they tried.

CHAPTER 11

Trauma Hidden in Plain Sight

We pulled up in front of the house on Hazel Street in Livermore late on a Saturday afternoon. Helmut had rented a cargo van to transport all my things. It was the first time any of my soon-to-be-ex caregivers had made sure all my personal belongings traveled with me. Helmut backed the van up to the garage, and we were greeted by Anne, the girls, and Anne's husband, Joe.

After we had unloaded the van, Helmut and Bruni drove away in stoic Germanic style. I think a long goodbye would have been too painful for them. I stood in the garage with the girls, and Anne helped as we unpacked my things and I settled into my new room.

As soon as the last box was unpacked, Anne announced I would be starting school on Monday. I was shocked. Normally, I got a week or so to get used to my environment. Anne laughed at my expression of surprise and said, "Not in this house, kiddo. Everyone goes to school right away."

To say moving from Marin County to Livermore was a culture shock for me would be an understatement. The two communities could not have been more different. Livermore was more of a blue-collar town, whereas Marin had been more educated and wealthier. In the early 1980s, Livermore had a population of about 50,000 people—considerably smaller than it is today—but still quite a bustling community. The Mirci family's house was part of a tract that included a number of other homes with kids. I soon learned to develop a friend group outside the home.

Both Anne and Joe had been educators in Livermore for many years by the time I came to live with them. He was a beloved principal, and she was a revered kindergarten teacher. From the outside, we had an idyllic family.

I knew I was likely to be quite the celebrity at my new school. Between the two of them, Anne and Joe knew a majority of the kids that were now my peers. Since I had taken their last name, the connection was instantaneous. Many times, I heard things like, "I had your dad in the third grade! He was the coolest teacher! You are so lucky!" or, "Your mom was the best teacher I've ever had. She's always so nice when I see her. She still remembers me after all this time!"

The night before the first day at my new school, Claudia and Maria dragged me into my bathroom to do my hair. Somewhere in the middle of all of the giggling, the curling iron scorched my forehead, but they managed to get my hair just the way they wanted it. Before I was even out of bed the following morning, they were at my bedroom door to style me for my grand debut.

I loved being back in public school after the small private school I had attended while living with Bruni and Helmut. At first, I was treated like a rock star by the girls. In the sixth grade, I was twelve years old and well into puberty. I was well-developed and had begun to lose my boyish features.

The boys, on the other hand, didn't take to me quite as readily. Although I had outgrown the effeminate preening of my earlier years, I was still far from stereotypically masculine. Livermore was still a rural town with less-than-liberal ideas of gender presentation.

After a month of living with the Mircis, I was informed by Anne that I would be expected to play a sport. She did not care what it was, but I had to pick something. Not playing a sport was not an option.

"Kids play sports," she said.

At first, I thought she was kidding. I was wrong. After a week, Anne asked me what sport I would like to play. I hadn't thought about it at all. This did not go over well. This was the first time Anne screamed at me. I would learn screaming was a blessing.

In the end, I did a short stint on the roller hockey team before Anne relented and realized it was not for me. She gave the topic of sports a rest for the time being.

I was pretty good at roller skating, though. I even convinced Anne to take me to the local roller rink where the school was holding an event. I was so excited, I put my skates on without even looking around and dashed out onto the rink. I was showing off all my best moves, doing spins, skating backwards, and thinking I was the coolest kid there when a girl skated up next to me.

She gave me a thorough onceover through narrowed eyes before asking, "Are you a girl?"

"Um...no. Why?"

"Because this is all-girls skate."

I looked around and I was the only boy on the rink. Everyone was staring at me, but not in the way I had hoped. I turned beet red. So much for being the coolest kid there.

While I much enjoyed the social aspect of school, the lack of effort I had shown while fighting Bruni over my homework began to show in my grades. Anne was not happy, and since she knew most of my teachers, there was no hiding my plummeting performance. When things spiraled out of control, I saw a side of Anne that would become all too familiar.

It began when my homeroom class teacher assigned a book report. I never mentioned the assignment to Anne and did as I had always done when it came to schoolwork—nothing. I read most of the book, but that's as far as it went. The day before the book report was due, Anne came home from work early and began to drill me with questions. She told me she had spoken to my teacher, and he had told her about the report. She wanted to see how far I had gotten, seeing as it was due the following day. When I told her I was still reading the book, a dark look came over her face. With no warning at all, she grabbed me by the hair and pulled. Her other hand struck me in the face. The sting of her slap buckled my knees, and I hit the tiled floor of the hall with a loud thud. She kept pulling my hair as I was on the floor and started kicking me and screaming, "WHAT DO YOU MEAN YOU'RE STILL READING? YOU WERE ASSIGNED THIS REPORT THREE WEEKS AGO! GET UP! GET UP YOU LAZY BASTARD!"

She still had a firm grip on my hair, and every time she spoke, she pulled harder. She dragged me into the dining room and threw me in a chair.

"I DON'T CARE IF WE ARE HERE ALL NIGHT LONG. YOU WILL FINISH THIS REPORT BEFORE YOU GO TO SCHOOL TOMORROW. NOW READ! AND DON'T MOVE UNTIL YOU'RE DONE! I DON'T CARE IF YOU SHIT YOUR PANTS!"

It took me about three hours to finish the rest of my book. When I had finished, Anne let me go to the bathroom. Once I was back at the table, she told me to start writing. When I thought I had finished my report, I told Anne. She came into the dining room, sat down, and started to read. As she was reading, her face twisted into a frown.

"What is this? Are you retarded? This is the worst report I have ever read!" She called out to Claudia, who had made herself scarce. "Claudia! Get me a red pen!" Her voice terrified me. It was as if she had become a different person. As Claudia handed Anne the pen, she shot me a look of warning.

When Anne finished editing my report, she threw it back in my face.

"This is SHIT! A third grader could write better than that! Do it over!"

I was terrified, exhausted, and couldn't stop crying. I must have looked confused or angry because she stood and snapped, "WIPE THAT LOOK OFF OF YOUR FACE BEFORE I KNOCK IT OFF!"

She stormed to the kitchen sink and began loading the dishwasher.

I became angry as well. Hadn't I done what she wanted? Now I was supposed to smile about it?

"What do you expect me to do, laugh?" I shouted after her.

Claudia's back was turned to Anne, but her eyes became the size of quarters and she cowered in her chair. I heard her say, "Uh-oh."

"WHAT DID YOU SAY?" Anne screeched from the kitchen sink. Her face was bright pink as she slammed the dishwasher door with all of her strength. The dishes she had been loading flew everywhere and shattered. The dishwasher door had been between where she stood and where I sat. In an instant she was towering over me. She grabbed my hair again and slammed my face down on the table.

"REEEAD! WHAT DOES IT SAY?" Her voice was back at a screech. Still, I was belligerent.

I said, "I don't know. It's too close. I can't see it."

Claudia thought this was funny and let out a chuckle in spite of herself.

Anne turned on her in an instant.

"Do you think that's funny?"

Claudia's eyes got wide again, and she hung her head. "No, Mom. I'm sorry."

Anne was still holding my hair. With one jerk she pulled my head backward until I was staring at the ceiling.

"REEEAD!" she screeched again.

I still had some defiance left in me. "How am I supposed to read it when all I can see is the ceiling?"

Wham! Wham! Wham! She slammed my face into the dining room table again and again.

"I SWEAR TO GOD, I'LL KILL YOU!"

Without warning, Anne grabbed my pencil and plunged it deep into my upper thigh. Perhaps the realization that she had just stabbed me brought her back to sanity because she turned on her heels and went back into the kitchen, barking at Claudia to help her clean up the mess she had made with the broken dishes.

The world seemed to freeze. I didn't know what to do. I sat there for what seemed like an eternity with a pencil sticking out of my thigh. The shocking suddenness of the attack was even more unnerving than the violence itself. I had been in abusive situations before, but the realization of just how unstable Anne was and how well she hid her manic violence from the world was more than my mind could handle.

"Mom?" Claudia spoke just above a whisper. "Don't you think we should put something on that?" Anne looked at me in disgust but grudgingly allowed Claudia to help me remove the pencil and clean my wound. She went up to her room for the night but not before she made it clear I was to finish my report—or else! Today I can still see the lead in my leg where Anne stabbed me.

Claudia did her best to arm me for the future as she sat and helped me clean my wound. She explained to me I should never talk back to Anne and that I had gotten off easy, considering my defiance. Anne wanted her kids to succeed and didn't care what she had to do to them to make it happen. That night, Claudia and I formed a close bond. The rest of the time I lived in Anne's house, I took on the role of protector, and there were many times I stepped in to divert Anne's attention from her to me. I often took beatings for Claudia and was happy to do it.

In the years that followed, there were many nights when I would sneak out of the house with a little bag and grand plans of running away. I never got more than half a mile before the thoughts of Claudia and Maria entered my head. I had developed a strong sense of responsibility for them, and I felt it was my duty to watch out for them. I always went back before anyone knew I had left. I would have never forgiven myself if anything happened to them and I was not there to protect them.

Despite what went on behind closed doors, Anne's public image as a successful teacher, loving wife, and caring mother was immaculate and carefully managed. There were many people who admired and respected

Anne, but there were few who truly knew her and almost none who loved her. I learned of her past in bits and pieces over the next few years, and it told a sadder story.

She had been raised in the South. She was a Southern belle, or so she liked to say. Her father was a prominent doctor in their town, and her mother had been a nurse. Anne spoke very little about her mother, and when she did, it was clear the relationship was tense at best. Anne always felt her mother had not wanted her. As a child, she had been close with her nanny, but her mother fired the nanny, blaming her when Anne contracted scarlet fever.

Anne's mother was rigid in her thinking and, although she tried to deny it, a flagrant racist. Anne had once taken Claudia and Maria to visit her. The girls were forbidden to sit on the furniture and were told to sit on the floor. Many years later, as we were cleaning out Anne's things after her death, I discovered a stack of letters between Anne and her mother. Anne had written numerous times, pleading with her mother to accept the girls as her grandchildren. The words her mother used in response were beyond hateful and offensive. When Anne wrote of me, her mother stated she had accepted me as her grandson simply because I was white. I never told the girls I found the letters. I shoved them all in the bottom of a garbage bag like the trash they were.

Despite appearances, Anne and her husband, Joe, also had a rocky relationship. I had never heard Helmut and Bruni exchange an angry word in the entire time I lived with them. Anne and Joe fought constantly.

Once, Joe came home after an evening out with friends and went upstairs to his room. It wasn't long before we heard the sound of shouting back and forth. The argument went on for about half an hour before their bedroom door flew open and Anne shrieked, "CALL THE POLICE! CALL 911! DAD JUST HIT ME!"

Maria dutifully dialed the police as Anne flew down the stairs screaming and waving her hands. Joe was hot on her tail, yelling at her to stop being so dramatic. A few minutes later, the police arrived. There was some conversation back and forth, and when the police felt everything was under control, they left. Joe came down the stairs and into the family room where we were all standing. The look on his face was pure anger. I was standing by the couch, Claudia on one side of me, Maria on the other.

Joe wasn't yelling at me, but the tone of his voice seemed deliberate, controlled, and very angry as he said, "You! Get out of my room!" He was referring to what was now my bedroom. Before I arrived, my room had been a place of refuge for him. He jabbed his index finger into my chest. "Get out. I want you out."

I was frozen in fear and didn't know what to do. He had never confronted me like that before. Anne stepped in and the two of them went back upstairs. The yelling and screaming continued for quite some time, but I didn't have to move out of my room.

In the years that I lived there, this was the only time Joe ever touched me. I believe his anger and frustration were the result of being forced into a situation he never asked for. Joe knew Anne was not a stable person, and I suspect after seeing what she had put the girls through, he was very resistant to the idea of taking on another child. She made no secret of the fact that she had always wanted a boy, and what she wanted, she usually got.

What Joe did not realize was that his actions that night affirmed everything Anne had told me about him—he hated me and resented me for "taking his place." Anne was a gifted manipulator. She knew how to play the victim and did it with exceptional cunning. Overall, Joe was not a very present member of our family, although he tried to be. I can hardly blame him.

The way she maligned Joe to me was typical of her tactics. The physical scars Anne left on my body pale in comparison to the emotional damage she did to all three of us kids. Anne seemed to take great pleasure in playing us against one another. We were all so eager to please her and stay out of her sights that we often turned on one another. When I first arrived at the Mirci home, I can remember finding it odd how often—at least twenty times per day—the girls told their mother they loved her.

"Love you", one of them would say and then wait for Anne's response. I soon learned this was how we could gauge Anne's mood. My hypervigilance told me everything I needed to know. We'd send out "love you" like emotional sonar to see what bounced back at us. I think this is part of the reason that, even today, I have such a hard time saying "I love you" to my mother.

If Anne took two of us shopping, the entire afternoon would be spent disparaging the one who was not present. We knew it was smart to join in the verbal bashing. She methodically created an atmosphere of suspicion and distrust, which she seemed to thrive on. Anne was never happier than when things were in chaos at home.

Worst of all the manipulations was how she tried to make me feel about Bruni. I realize now that she was jealous of the stabilizing and loving influence Bruni had given me. Anne told me Bruni was "perverted" and had been trying to molest me when she would lie with me at night as a little boy. I heard this over and over, but I never believed it. She told me I had been so terrible that Helmut and Bruni had to get rid of me because they couldn't take it anymore. She told me it was my fault that Helmut had died. She said he would have been able to fight his cancer, but because I was such a hateful child, he was too weak after dealing with me. This statement stuck with me well into adulthood. It was not until I was thirty-five years old, sitting at Bruni's dining room table, that I learned the real reason for me leaving their home.

Before I was placed with her, Anne was given access to all the information that had been compiled on me. She knew everything about every placement I had ever been in. This is standard procedure when placing a foster child. Prospective foster parents are given as much information as possible about the children they are to care for. The logic behind this is to give foster parents some insight into the child so that they can better understand potential behavioral issues. Anne used this information as a weapon. She knew exactly where to hit. I had never given much thought to the fact that Kathy and Leo had chosen to adopt C.C. and not me. In my mind it was a good fit. Anne had another opinion. When she was feeling particularly vengeful, she said, "You were such an awful little shit that Kathy and Leo chose a nigger kid over you!" It was Anne who introduced me to open prejudice and bigotry. I had never heard that word before I lived with her. When she spoke of C.C. like this it hurt me deeply and she knew it. As much as she tried to hide it, she had not escaped the indoctrination of her mother's racist household unscathed.

CHAPTER 12

The Paradox of Abusive Stability

My life in the Mirci household was not all bad. As damaged as it was, in some ways it was just what I needed.

Once my schoolwork was up to par in Anne's eyes, she once again brought up the issue of playing a sport. Track season was upon us, and both Claudia and Maria were on the Catholic Youth Organization track team, which made it the logical option. Still, I was not excited to go to my first practice. Anne introduced me as her son, as she always did, and told the coach I had decided to give this "track thing" a shot. The coach gave me an appraising eye and seemed satisfied.

"Well—let's see what he can do. You ever run a 100-yard sprint before, kid?"

"Uh…nope," I said. A hundred yards might as well have been a mile.

Anne pinched the back of my upper arm as hard as she could.

"OUCH! What was that for?" I asked.

"Nope?" she hissed. "What kind of answer is that?" I looked at her in confusion. She sighed and elaborated. "You will respond with respect when spoken to by an adult. Is that clear? The appropriate response would have been *no, sir.*" From that day forward, my track coach was "sir." I still have no idea what his name was.

When Anne had finished correcting me, the coach told me to get onto the track. He lined me up with several other boys my age, all of whom were wearing shorts and running shoes. I fumbled trying to position my feet in the blocks and my hands on the track until the coach showed me how to do it. I felt like a giraffe on stilts. I was the tallest and least coordinated of the boys lining up on the chalk.

The coach stepped away from the line. "On your marks!............Get set!...........GO!" The coach barely got the word "go" out of his mouth before I was out of the blocks and running with every ounce of strength and energy I could muster. As I raced down the track, I felt complete freedom. I was alone and in charge of my own destiny. In the few seconds it took me to get to the finish line, the outside world turned off and no one could say anything to me. I was hooked. When I crossed the finish line, panting, and looked up to see who else was there, I fully expected to see the other boys standing around waiting for me. I was shocked to discover I was alone. The second-place kid took another few seconds to cross and the rest caught up after that. I had outdistanced them by a wide margin. Anne looked at me with a combination of pride and shock as if she didn't know who I was. Coach just made a mark on his clipboard. "Well—I guess we found a new sprinter."

Anne looked at me, beamed, and said, "I guess so!"

That tryout on the track was my first experience with the feeling of pride. Before that, I had never felt good at anything. The knowledge I had succeeded on my own merits—that others were genuinely impressed, not because it was charitable, but because I had earned their respect—was foreign to me. Most surprising was that it had come with so little effort. I barely broke a sweat and could have done it again. I spent the rest of the afternoon running, sprinting, and, best of all, winning!

The following day, I woke up and could hardly move. Since I had never been involved in any kind of sport before, I had no idea how achy you could get the next day. My introduction into the world of muscle pain caused no end of amusement for Anne and the girls.

From the very beginning, Anne expected more from me. She often told me, since Joe was never around, I was going to have to be the man of the house. I was expected to do well in school—period. No one had ever set high standards for me before. This was to become the paradoxical theme of my life with Anne—despite the constant abuse, manipulation, and degradation, there was a sense that it was all to make me better. Whatever else may have been wrong in her mind, her belief in my ability to achieve excellence was ironclad, and she would force me to believe in myself by whatever means necessary.

The first few months, I did not do very well in school, despite the beatings. One Saturday morning, Anne got me out of bed very early. "Get up!" she ordered. I had learned not to question her, so I did as I was told and got dressed. As she bundled me into the car in the cold morning air, she said, "I don't know what's going on with you and school, but I'm not going to beat a dead horse. We're going on a little trip."

We drove from Livermore all the way back to Marin County in silence. The drive seemed to take forever. Eventually, we arrived at a modern-looking building. Anne told me to wait in the lobby and soon returned with a young woman in tow. My first thought was that I was about to get dumped again, but my ever-present instinctual alarms were quiet. Whatever was happening, it might not be a bad thing. The young woman introduced herself and told me I was going to be given a series of tests. The rest of the morning and the afternoon seemed to drag on forever. At least the tests weren't too hard. Most of them featured multiple-choice questions about shapes or figuring out the next picture in a sequence. I finished well before the allotted time. When I handed back the last one, I was taken back out to the lobby where Anne was waiting for me. The entire drive home Anne did not say a word to me.

The following week, we repeated the exercise. Anne drove me back to the facility in Marin. We waited in the lobby for a little while, and the same young woman appeared and handed Anne a binder. The woman offered to explain it, but Anne cut her off and said she was well versed in this particular subject. When the woman left, Anne flipped open the binder and began to read it. She grunted a few times and gasped several more but never spoke. I knew better than to say anything, so I sat across from her studying her face as she read. Every once in a while, she looked up and at me with an unpleasant expression.

When she had finished reading the contents of the binder, she calmly closed it and scooted forward in her chair, beckoning me to do the same. I leaned in, eager to know what the results of the test were and sure I had done well. As soon as I was in striking distance, Anne's palm swung around and connected with my face with incredible force. It stunned me more than hurt me. I had no idea what was going on.

"What? Why? What did I do?" I cried.

"I'm only going to say this once, so you'd better listen, mister. If you EVER, I mean EVER, get a grade lower than a B in your life again, I'll kill you!"

I knew she was serious and believed she really would kill me. From that day on, I got straight As in school. To this day, I don't know what the results of my IQ tests were. Anne never told me. The only clue she ever gave me was when I would do something she felt was stupid or childish. She would say, "You have an IQ that is practically higher than both of your sisters combined. Act like it or else!"

As an adult, I often wonder where my life would have taken me without the structure, however brutal, she provided. Bruni had adored me and made me feel safe and secure, but the direction I was headed while living with her was nothing short of catastrophic. I was failing in school, had no sense of self, no sense of responsibility, and no respect for anything or anyone. I was a wild child.

Would I have outgrown my problematic behavior with Bruni as my mother? Would I have learned how important school was and lived up to my potential? Maybe. Obviously, no child should ever be beaten, but these questions underscore the complexity of the relationship I shared with Anne and the girls. No matter what Anne did to me, one thing that was always crystal clear was that she loved me and would stand by me no matter what. Where Bruni gave hope, Anne gave structure and, ultimately, success. A home like that, no matter how broken, was more steadfast and reliable than any I had known.

As I began to adjust to my new life as a competent student and active preteen, I began to feel something I had never felt before: settled. Life with Anne was no picnic, but something in me recognized what I had in this family. I wouldn't call it stability, but it was consistency. The combination of a family, frightening as it may have been, and the support of the community brought a new me to the surface.

As time went on, my grades became stronger and stronger. I earned a spot on the honor roll every semester. I discovered school was quite easy when I put the effort in. I learned to balance my schoolwork with track and, later, tennis. We belonged to the town's private tennis club and were expected to attend lessons, rain or shine. At first, I hated it but came to discover I had some talent for that as well. Livermore can get as hot as 110 degrees in the summer, and we were expected to ride our bikes across town and spend at least four days a week at the club. In spite of the heat, I didn't mind the discomfort because it gave me some freedom and time away from the house.

I struggled daily with the conflict of my deepening love and devotion to my sisters, being an upstanding member of a community, my love for Anne, and what I knew was not a normal or healthy family life. I finally had what I had wanted throughout my childhood. I was part of a family—such as it was. I had friends, a place in the world, and even a hint that I was worthy of a brighter future.

Throughout this time, I remained close with Bruni, and she often came to visit and went on trips with us. Although she was delighted to see the young man I was becoming, she struggled with her own feelings of failure in knowing I would never have developed this way had I stayed with her. Of course, she had no idea what was going on behind closed doors. It would be many years before I spoke to her about it and she truly understood the extent of Anne's abuse. When I first told her, she didn't even believe me. Anne was such a different person in public than she was in private that I can see why it was difficult for Bruni.

When she was proud of something one of us had done, Anne could make us feel incredibly special. She loved to drive and would often take us on road trips, sometimes with Bruni or other friends in tow. These trips often included laughter, antics, and family bonding that made all of us kids feel loved and wanted. On one such adventure, I threw a can of beans in the fire because I was too tired to grab a pot and, being a teenage boy, didn't think it through. The can exploded, of course. Claudia's boyfriend at the time was even nicked by a piece of bean-can shrapnel, but instead of blaming or reprimanding me, Anne laughed it off and we all exchanged good-natured jokes about the "bean bomb" incident for the rest of the trip.

The summer I turned thirteen, Anne sent me to wilderness survival camp as part of her endless mission to "butch me up." The camp was run by an older Indigenous man named Crow, but I really connected with one of the camp advisors, Bruce, who was also a Casey Family social worker.

When I got to the parking lot where we were all meeting for the camp bus, I was lugging a heavy bag. Bruce asked to look inside and was soon pulling out all the "essentials" I had packed, including a hair dryer, a book light, and tons of other useless stuff. I was mortified, but he took it in stride, and we all laughed about it. Bruce and I formed a bond on that trip.

At camp, we slept in a teepee and Crow taught us how to survive off the land, build fires, and find edible plants before we were to hike up a mountain as the "grand finale." The majesty of the final stay atop the mountain was somewhat undercut. I woke up to see Crow, shirtless, banging two pots together and yelling while a chagrined black bear made a hasty retreat from our food supply. I don't know if it made me any more "butch," but survival camp was a highlight of my teenage years, and I have Anne to thank for it.

As I entered eighth grade, I began to excel even more at track. Anne never missed a track meet. There could be hundreds of people in the stands watching, but I could always hear Anne's voice screaming at me to run faster. With few exceptions, I came in first place. To this day, I can hear her voice in the back of my head as I am running. It doesn't matter if I have run ten miles and am completely exhausted, I always sprint all-out the last quarter mile.

CHAPTER 13

The Impact of Mental Health

It wasn't long before I realized Anne had deeper problems than just her need for physical and emotional chaos and her uncontrollable anger. From the moment she came home from work and for the rest of the evening, she always seemed to have a glass of wine in her hand. As the evening progressed, she became more and more relaxed. I started noticing the number of bottles of wine she bought when we went grocery shopping together. The recycling can we used for glass containers became so heavy, I often had to ask Claudia to help me drag it to the curb. As we tilted it up onto the sidewalk, we heard the clink of wine bottles. We looked at its contents and then looked back up at one another. Although no words were exchanged, we both realized in that moment that Anne's drinking was becoming a problem, or so I thought.

One night, after Anne had consumed a significant amount of wine, Claudia was in my room asking me something, and I said, "Hey—I think Mom's drunk."

"What? No, she's not," Claudia snapped.

I thought she was joking with me. "Are you serious?" I asked. "Come on. She drove up the curb on our way home! Watch her. Listen to her when she talks." By this point in the evening, Anne's speech was noticeably slurred. I couldn't understand how Claudia missed what was going on until I realized she and Maria had spent their entire lives watching this.

"You're being stupid," she stated and left my room in a huff. I thought that was the end of it.

About half an hour later, I was sitting on the toilet when the bathroom door flew open. Anne was standing in the doorway, hair looking like she had just come in from a rainstorm and eyes crazed with anger. She had to brace herself in the doorframe as she screamed, "Why did you tell your sister I am drunk?"

I knew no matter what I said I was going to get it, so I figured I might as well be honest. "I thought you were, Mom. You're slurring when you talk, and you look like you can barely stand up."

Before I could say another word, Anne had me by the hair and started to pull me off the toilet, but I couldn't let her pull me off before I finished what I had started or I would risk crapping on myself. I chose to fight her off long enough to finish, but in the process, a half inch of my scalp was ripped from my head. When the hair and skin came off in her hand, Anne stumbled backwards and hit the doorknob.

"FUCK! That hurt! C'mere, you little fucker!" The drunker Anne got, the worse her language became. She came at me like a bulldozer and grabbed me by the hair again. "I'll rip every fucking hair out of your head, you little shit! Get out here!"

I was now off of the toilet and on my knees. I had learned from past experience that by tilting my head in the direction she was pulling and going along with the yank, the pain was not as bad. I was too big for Anne to throw me through the air as Mother had done, but that didn't stop her from trying. I was in the small hallway between my bedroom and my bathroom in a flash.

"GET ON YOUR KNEES, YOU LITTLE FUCKER!" Anne was still holding my hair with one hand as she began to slap me repeatedly with the other. Not satisfied with that, she began kicking as well. Claudia and Maria stood off to the side and watched in horror. It lasted only a few minutes, but a few minutes is enough to inflict a lot of damage. When she was finished, she barked at me to stay in my room for the rest of the night.

"I don't want to look at'cher ugly face!"

I learned that night never to speak of Anne's drinking again. In time, Claudia and then Maria each became more aware there was a problem. All three of us had an unspoken language of signals and glances to warn one another of just how drunk Anne happened to be at any moment.

Sometimes when Anne was drunk, she was great fun to be around, smiling and laughing and very relaxed. More often than not, however, she became mean and savagely violent. On one occasion, she sat me at the kitchen table and kept hitting me. She thought it was funny and giggled with the girls at her side. I was going to be starting high school in a year and a half, and she said the kids in high school would "kick my ass." She felt that by punching me and slapping me over and over I would become tougher and "more prepared." I was not permitted to cry and complain. If I did, she hit me harder and faster. Anne seemed to take a great deal of pleasure in my agony. To keep from being her next target, the girls had no choice but to go along with, and even join in, my torment.

When Joe came home and saw what was going on, he grabbed Anne's hand as it was in midair for yet another blow.

"I think he's had enough. Don't you?" he said.

This was not the first time Joe had been my savior. There were many times he stepped in and pulled her off of me or one of the girls. By then, Anne had me convinced he didn't like me, and it was best for me to stay away from him. She could be extremely persuasive, but looking back, he was not at all the person she made him out to be.

The first week of seventh grade was marked by the worst beating I had ever received. Anne always gave us lunch money, but there was also a pile of quarters on the china hutch that were to be used for the bus and only for the bus. One morning Anne forgot to leave my lunch money, so I took some extra quarters to pay for my lunch. That evening, as I was doing my homework in my room, I heard the shrill sound of Anne's drunken voice resonate through the house. She was calling my name. I knew that tone very well by now and I expected that, at best, I would lose some hair. I went up to the kitchen and presented myself.

"Where are all of the quarters?" Anne asked in a crazed tone. I breathed a sigh of relief, thinking it would be easy to set this one straight.

"Oh, I took some extra ones because you forgot to leave my lunch money." I said, feeling confident she would realize I had no other option.

"THIEF!" "THIEF!" Anne shrieked at me.

"What? No, Mom, I didn't......" was the last coherent thing I said.

That year, I not only wore glasses, but also braces with full headgear and matching neck-gear. Anne grabbed the straps attached to my gear and ripped it out of my mouth, slicing the inside of my cheeks in the process. The pain was so intense I felt as if I was going to pass out.

She looked down in drunken surprise at the straps and wires dangling from her hand and the blood dripping on the floor. She hadn't expected it to come free. She grunted and threw it across the kitchen before going for her old favorite—my hair. The moment I felt her pulling my hair from my scalp, I hit the floor with a thud like a sack of potatoes. Still clinging to my hair, she began to strike me in the face and chest with her fist while continuing to chant "THIEF! THIEF!"

I begged her to stop, but that only made her hit harder and faster. I had become accustomed to the smell of Rhine wine on her breath. She bought it in two-gallon jugs—at least four or five a week. This particular evening, something was different. The smell of Rhine wine had been replaced with another, stronger smell, as if she had been drinking gasoline. I later learned she had graduated to vodka.

In trying to get away from the onslaught of blows and continued yanking on my hair, I had unknowingly edged closer to the stairs. She started kicking me in the stomach so hard it knocked the wind out of me. As I was gasping to catch my breath, I could feel myself go over the edge. I tumbled to the bottom in a heap. Anne chased me down the stairs and reached for my hair again. She was still screaming "THIEF! THIEF!" despite being winded from her efforts. She dragged me along the floor to the entrance to my bedroom. She tried to drag me in, but the transition from linoleum to carpet made it too difficult.

"GET UP! GET UP AND GET IN THERE!" she said.

As I jumped to my feet and entered my room, her left fist came out of nowhere and connected to my nose. I fell onto my bed, bleeding.

Still screaming "THIEF," she began to throw whatever she could out of my bedroom door. Claudia had come to see what was going on. She stood and stared in astonishment. The look on her face—a combination of terror and pity—told me she had never seen Anne become so violent, but she also knew better than to say a word. One by one, Anne managed to throw nearly every item out of my bedroom door. My alarm clock hit Claudia in the head. When I thought there was nothing else for her to throw out the bedroom door, she looked me and said, "GET UP! GET OFF THAT BED!" She struggled to lift the full-size mattress from the box spring.

"You want to steal from me, kiddo, then I'll steal from you." She threw the mattress into the hall, followed by the box spring. The only thing left for her to throw was my dresser.

Anne was not a large woman. She stood about five feet six inches high. Her drinking had added some additional weight, but I was at least three to four inches taller than she was. Still, I was terrified of her as she stood over me, huffing and puffing. In a calm, steely tone, she said, "Don't you ever take anything in this house without asking first. I don't care if you're dying or starving. If I say you can't have it, then don't touch it. You got that?"

I grunted and nodded.

"Good—now clean up this mess." As she navigated her way through her handiwork, she looked at Claudia and said, "I have to go pick up your sister. Claudia Mirci, if you help your brother clean up this mess, I'll kill you!"

Then she was gone. As drunk as she was, she drove across town to pick up Maria.

Once we were sure it was safe, Claudia came into my room and put her arms around me. I wish I could say this was the last time Anne beat me, but I can say it was the worst of it.

After the incident with the quarters, Claudia and I reached out to Kathee and told her what was going on. She struggled with the information. Sometimes social workers have difficulty believing the words of kids who are known for acting out or just being dramatic, and Anne had perfected her respectable facade. But with Claudia and I both corroborating each other, Kathee was left with a bigger problem: what to do next. She knew the challenges I was facing with Anne, but also knew Anne loved me and was setting me up for success. The statistics did not bode well for me if I returned to the system and bounced from home to home. My odds of a healthy adulthood would have plummeted. In the end, she left it up to me and I chose to stay with Anne. Kathee arranged for some steps to be taken with hopes of "revising" Anne's behavior, but none of us knew how far gone she was at that point.

It was one of the many difficult calls Kathee had to make as a social worker with extremely limited resources. We reconnected when I was in my twenties and she said she had always felt bad about leaving me there, but I reassured her it was the right thing to do. After four years with the Casey Family Program, she moved into another career. She simply cared too much and got burned out. It was a thankless role of tremendous responsibility and limited power with the lives of children at stake. Social workers were, and still are, asked to do so much with so little. Bureaucracy and lack of funding hamper them at every turn. There often isn't a good answer, and they have to do the best they can with the options they have.

Sometime during my seventh-grade year, Kathee left the Casey Family Program, although she still made time to come to my eighth-grade graduation. A jovial older Black woman named Faye White became my new social worker. Faye was fun and funny and lived in the Oakland hills. One of her neighbors was the former child star Shirley Temple Black. We would sometimes hang out at Shirley's house, and I met her on a couple of occasions. I suppose it was my brush with fame, but we always got a kick out of the irony of their last names.

CHAPTER 14

The Power of Community

The summer before I started high school, the family learned Joe had been having a long-time affair with a woman named Gladys, whom he had met in Utah. He had traveled there frequently to visit his family and to get away from Anne and their endless fights. When the affair came to light, Joe was honest about the situation and answered all our questions. It was a relief to me and the girls that he had found someone. He and Anne had not been happy for a long time. Joe explained to us that he was going to leave but we were always welcome to phone him or even visit if we wanted to. He encouraged us to call if we needed anything at all. This was the first time I got a sense that Joe might not be the monster Anne had made him out to be.

Something in Anne shifted when the reality of life without Joe sank in. For most of that summer, the tight leash she had previously kept on me was forgotten. I came and went as I pleased, and she said nothing about it. She began to drink even more than usual and started going to bed earlier, so we saw less of her as the summer went on.

Most of the kids I graduated from junior high with went on to Livermore High, but Anne had decided I would be better off at the high school across town, Granada High. I was devastated at the time, but it turned out to be a good decision. Livermore High was a bit of a hick school. Their mascot was the cowboy. The guys all wore jeans and T-shirts every day. Granada was in a wealthier, more educated area. They had more progressive values and more emphasis on art and culture. Let's just say that, for a pretty, somewhat effeminate boy, it was a better fit. I felt at ease right away and made friends quickly. I knew some of the kids already through Catholic catechism as well as through track and basketball. I started to enjoy myself.

The summer before high school was also when she stopped hitting me. Shortly after I graduated from junior high, I was in trouble for something, and Anne was screaming and yelling as usual, but now something was different. I could sense she was weaker, and I had grown much stronger. As Anne lifted her hand to strike me, I grabbed her wrist.

"No," I said. "No more. If you hit me again, I'll hit you back." My tone was calm, but she knew I meant it. She never touched me again.

Even Anne's attempts at psychological abuse started to backfire. By the time I graduated from junior high, I had, for the first time in my life, a significant number of friends. At one point, a group of us were busted for joyriding in some of our parents' cars. A week or two later, some of the girls I knew tried it again and were involved in a minor accident. My name was at the top of the list as an instigator, and I became persona non grata among my friends' parents practically overnight. So much so, that barely anyone would talk to me at school for fear of parental wrath. In truth, I had not been involved in the second incident at all, but when Anne heard about it, she seethed.

Knowing she could no longer beat me, she tried her second favorite tactic, reputation sabotage. She dug through my bedroom and found my address book. One by one, she called my friends' parents and spewed horrific things about me: I was a psychopath, a sociopath, a pathological liar, and a fag. I had been in trouble for molesting small children. She went on and on.

The result was the exact opposite of what she had intended. All the parents she called were shocked at how unhinged she was and developed a greater capacity for sympathy and understanding where I and my behavior were concerned. I later found out that there was a flurry of calls around the neighborhood to discuss how to protect me from "that crazy woman." Even parents whose children did not know me started to gather for my cause. Unknown to me, the community had claimed me as one of their own. Just as quickly as I had become the neighborhood pariah, I was approached and welcomed into the homes of my friends again. Of course, I wasn't aware of Anne's actions and their consequences at the time. I just knew I had been on the outs with the community and then was welcomed back. It was odd, but I had too many other things on my mind to question it.

I had started modeling by happenstance around this time. A friend took a few pictures of me for fun and sent some to a competition at the local shopping mall without my knowledge. The mall called and asked me to compete in a promotional fashion show they were putting on. I had to lie about my age and say I was sixteen to get in, but I ended up winning and doing several photo shoots for them. This landed me an agent and a few local gigs here and there. I never made much money from it, but it contributed a great deal to my confidence and made me something of a celebrity at my new school, particularly among the girls.

As I felt my fortunes starting to rise, Anne's were falling. She started to slide further and further away from us. It wasn't long after I started high school that the police arrived at our front door. They said they had received a call from a concerned neighbor and there was a suicide watch out on Anne. I was confused. She had always taught us suicide was the coward's way out. When Joe came to the door to see what was going on, the police asked him to get Anne. When she refused to come down from her room, they went up to see her.

I was filled with red-hot rage. Through all the manipulation and abuse, all the hidden trauma, the drinking, the smear campaigns, and the screaming, I had known one thing to be true: Anne would never abandon us. She would never make us feel unwanted. The very idea of her attempting suicide or even thinking about it was more of a betrayal than all the rest.

I packed a bag and stormed out. I walked to a friend's house a few miles away and asked if I could stay there for a few days. They agreed, but only if I called home first.

It was Joe who convinced me to return. In a gentle, kind tone, he told me the girls needed me, and I needed to be with them. He came and picked me up to take me home, but I didn't stay home long. As we sat together in my room, I told him why I was so angry. Joe explained Anne was having a hard time dealing with the breakup of their marriage and she was crying out for help.

As we were talking, there was a gentle knock on my door and then Anne appeared. She was wearing her bathrobe, her hair was sticking straight up, and her face was puffy from alcohol and tears. She spoke in a broken tone I had never heard before.

"What are you talking about in here?"

"WHAT DO YOU THINK?" I yelled. It was the first time I had ever raised my voice to her, and I didn't hold back my rage. "What is wrong with you? Do you have any idea how it feels to answer the door to the police and learn there is a suicide watch on your mother? Do you even care?"

She stared at her feet. "Well, what do I have to live for?"

I went white with rage. "YOU STUPID SELFISH BITCH! WHAT THE FUCK ARE CLAUDIA, MARIA, AND I? WE AREN'T WORTH LIVING FOR? FUCK YOU TOO!"

I stormed past her and out of the house. I stayed with another friend and didn't come home for a while.

For the next few weeks, Anne was like a different person. She went to work but she was always in her room when I got home. Every day after school, I found a gift on my bed: a new jacket, new shirt, pants, shoes, a radio. Every day, I took the item upstairs and threw it at her bedroom door. Every day, she poked her head out and mumbled the same question.

"You don't like it?"

Every day, I spat the same response over my shoulder. "No, I don't want it. I want you. Get your shit together or leave me alone!"

This gift-giving ritual went on through the first few weeks of my freshman year of high school. Anne hid in her room and drank more and more.

One day I came home to find Anne's car was not in the driveway. I went inside and found Maria sitting on the stairs with her face buried in a letter. Claudia was standing off to the side with tears in her eyes. My heart sank. I was sure Anne had killed herself.

"Mom's gone," Claudia said. "She left." She extended the letter, and I scanned it as fast as I could.

> *Dear Kids –*
> *I have some things I need to work through. I am taking some time to do some soul searching. I've gone up the coast and will be back in a week or two…*

The two-page letter ended with a special note to me:

> *Gino – Take care of your sisters. You're the man of the house now.*

Joe was still living with us from time to time as he attempted to extricate his belongings, figure out the finances, and deal with all the other logistical issues that come with a divorce. When he arrived home that day, I handed over the letter. He took his time to read through it twice before telling us not to worry. He assured us Anne would be fine. She just needed to take some time. He would stay with us until she got back. He also told us not to mention anything about it to anyone outside the house. News travels fast in a small town, and the story could damage her professional credibility as a teacher. The three of us agreed and tried to sweep it under the rug for the time being.

The next week, I was standing in the kitchen when the phone rang.

"Hello! Hello! Is Joe there, please?" The woman sounded panicked.

"May I ask who's calling?" I replied.

"Oh—um, this is Janet, I'm—um, Gladys's daughter. Something's happened. I have to speak to Joe immediately!"

When I told Joe who was on the phone, he snatched the receiver from my hand before I could finish. I studied his face as he spoke to the woman on the line.

"OH MY GOD! NO! Is she okay?" Joe's face was ashen. "I'll get there as soon as I can!"

He hung up the phone and turned to me. "Your mother just shot Gladys. She's in surgery right now. I have to go to Utah. Your mother is fine, but she's in jail."

We later learned the trip of "working things out" involved buying a gun, rope, trash bags, a pickaxe, a shovel, a cattle prod, and gloves and driving to Utah with the intention of "attacking" Gladys. When she arrived at the house, Anne had found Gladys was not at home but was able to break in. While waiting for Gladys to arrive, Anne, in her diminished mental state, decided to take a bath and fell asleep in the tub. When Gladys arrived to find a strange woman in her bathtub, she screamed. This woke Anne up. They struggled over the gun, which Anne had brought with her into the bathroom, and it went off, shooting Gladys. She was wounded but managed to escape the house and call the authorities. Meanwhile, Anne had fled the scene and drove to Las Vegas. From there she called a friend from Livermore, who flew out to try and help her. This is where the police caught up with her and found all the suspicious equipment in her car.

It was a mess.

Joe was now left to deal with his mentally ill wife, wounded lover, and Anne's kids—which is what the three of us were. Joe had never wanted to adopt. It had always been Anne who wanted us, but now he was stuck with us. At least he was stuck with Claudia and Maria, who had been legally adopted, but my adoption had not been finalized. Joe was desperate to minimize the number of responsibilities on his plate, and I was more than ready to leave. I called a friend's parents, and they said I could come stay with them. As Joe was driving me to their house, he told me I was not, under any circumstances, to tell anyone what had happened. I was to say it was "a family emergency." The truth would be all over the papers soon enough.

The next few days at school were difficult. I became very withdrawn, always on the verge of tears and afraid to speak to anyone. I was able to hold it in for three days until Mrs. Whanlyn's first-period English class.

One of my female friends sat next to me. She knew me well enough to sense something was troubling me. We were in the middle of silent reading when she leaned over to me and whispered, "Are you okay? Come on. You can tell me. I'm your friend," in a tone so caring and sincere that I could no longer hold back my emotions. My tears burst forth and I cried in great gulping sobs. Mrs. Whanlyn looked up from her desk and asked me if I needed to step outside. I shook my head. By now the entire class was looking at me, which just made it even worse.

When the bell rang, Mrs. Whanlyn excused the class and asked me to stay behind. She did her best to get me to talk about what was bothering me. I refused. She sent me to the school counselor, but I refused to talk with her either. I said I would be fine.

Then I went home to Anne's house and started cleaning. In addition to being an alcoholic, Anne suffered from obsessive compulsive hoarding. She could not part with anything, so our house was always cluttered and filthy. I spent most of the afternoon cleaning and scrubbing. I threw away as much as I could fit in the garbage cans. When I was done, I looked around at my work. I had all but eliminated every trace of Anne. Not so much as a picture could be seen of her except for one oil painting from downstairs, which I hung above the couch in the living room. I knew it was only a matter of time before the story hit the newspapers, and I did not want to be ashamed when people came to our house.

Two days later, the story of the shooting was on the front page. I knew everyone was staring at me as I walked down the hallways at school. Mrs. Whanlyn even expressed her heartfelt concern and told me that if I needed anything, I should ask. I thanked her, but inside I was still in shock.

At the end of class as we all filed out, I was surprised to see the principal waiting for me. He motioned for me to join him and put his arm around my shoulder. As we were walking to his office, he said, "You are one popular young man!"

When we got to the office, he gently closed the door and told me the phone had been ringing all morning.

"In all of my years as a school administrator, I've never seen such an outpouring of support in a time of crisis," he said.

I assumed this outpouring was for our family. I said, "Well, a lot of people in town know who my parents are, so it doesn't surprise me they would be supportive of us."

"Maybe I wasn't clear enough. The calls we have been getting all morning were calls specifically for you. I've never seen anything like it. You are a very fortunate young man."

"Me? Why me?" I asked, unsure what all this meant.

I had only skimmed through the article in the newspaper earlier that morning. I had missed that it had mentioned one of Mrs. Mirci's children had not been legally adopted and was still technically a foster child. It didn't mention me by name, but in our small town, it was no secret who was the youngest and newest member of the Mirci household.

The principal handed me a stack of messages, saying, "See, these are all for you. Every one of these people has offered you a place to live."

One by one I flipped through the messages. This had to be some kind of mistake. There were at least twenty. Many were the parents of friends from the track team, but there were also messages from people I didn't know well. There was even one from Mrs. Dolan, who had been my yard-duty attendant in junior high. I hadn't even seen her other than at school or at church. She was always very kind and complimentary, but now she was offering me an open-ended invitation to stay with her family for as long as I wanted.

Anne's attempted slander campaign had ironically set the stage for this outpouring of goodwill. It had been the clue to her mental illness for the neighborhood. The shooting had only solidified their support and given them a reason to rally to my side. At the time, though, all I knew was that it was overwhelming. I handed back all the messages but one.

"Thanks," I said, "but I have a place to live. My mom will be back."

Deep down I knew it wasn't true. I had saved Mrs. Dolan's message just in case.

In all the craziness surrounding the shooting, Mrs. White suggested I move into another foster home. I agreed to meet the family, but the second I crossed the threshold, the hairs on the back of my neck stuck straight up. I was fifteen now, but the old alarm bells were still alive and well. I could almost smell the fake, smarmy atmosphere of a for-profit foster "family." The front door opened into a perfectly manicured living room—spotless with vintage settees swaddled in clear plastic. A three-foot-wide plastic runway directed visitors from the front door through the living room and into the family area of the home behind louvered, white accordion doors that were kept shut. Mrs. Roberts was in her mid to late fifties with short, reddish blond hair coifed within an inch of its life. She wore a floral muumuu and spoke with a slight Southern accent. Her appearance may have seemed harmless to most people, but I could feel the unctuous smugness coming off her in waves.

Mr. Roberts was older than Mrs. Roberts by at least ten years. He was a large man who struck me as gruff and quiet. I could tell right away that Mrs. Roberts was the disciplinarian and ruled the house with an iron fist. As we walked through the accordion doors, the alarm bells in my head were deafening. The staircase had at least ten senior portraits going all the way up. These were but a small sample of the kids that had come through their doors. Hanging above the TV like a trophy was their foster care license for all to see. "The Roberts Home for Children, license number…" I was appalled. I was used to being in a home with a family and community. This place might have more of a veneer of humanity than the Dependent Unit or 601 Unit, but I knew an institution when I saw one.

As we were leaving, Mrs. Roberts handed me a business card with "The Roberts Home for Children" and her name embossed on the bottom: Wava Roberts.

When we got in the car, I looked at Mrs. White with tears in my eyes and said, "NO." She gave me a nod of agreement, but a week later, she called to tell me the Roberts were very excited that I would be coming.

"Um, no. That's not happening," I said flatly.

"Gino, you don't have a choice. If you want to stay in Livermore, you have to move there. They are the only licensed foster parents in the area."

"What about the Dolans?" I asked.

I had gone to visit the Dolans not long before we went to see the Roberts. Joyce was chipper and boisterous. She had always adored me as a kid, she said. Her husband, Ken, was quiet and gentle—a complete contrast to Joyce. He had a calming way about him that put me at ease. I had spent my entire childhood fearing men, but in Ken I found an adult man I could trust. However apprehensive I may have been, I knew the Dolans were my only hope of staying in the town that had become my home. The alternative was tantamount to starting over, once again becoming an unwanted product of an unfeeling system.

"They aren't licensed," Mrs. White said. "The Roberts really are our only option right now…things being as they are."

It was in that moment I resolved to stand up for myself. I was done staring at my shoes and keeping my mouth shut. The rage I had suppressed and kept under control since I was little broke through in a rush. If no one else was going to advocate for me, I would do it myself.

"That's not my problem!" I shouted into the phone. "I'm done being treated like an animal. You can't just stick me wherever you want! I have never complained because I always felt like I was to blame for every failed placement. This is not my fault! I want to be with the Dolans. Get them a fucking license!" I slammed the phone down. I felt bad for yelling at her and terrified for what the future might hold, but I also felt a tremendous sense of empowerment. I was finding my voice.

The next two or three days were filled with tremendous anxiety. Would I be pulled from my friends and my school and shipped off somewhere to start over with who knows what kind of family? As I was walking in the front door from school a few days later, the phone rang. I answered to hear Mrs. White on the other end. She sounded elated.

"Okay, Gino, I heard you," she said. "We had to move mountains, but we got approval to move you in with the Dolans while they get their foster care license. You move next weekend."

"Thank you," I said. "I'll start packing."

CHAPTER 15

Forgiveness & Letting Go

Amid the chaos surrounding the shooting and during the following two years with the Dolans, my biological parents made a reappearance in my life. That same manic summer before my freshman year of high school, I had gotten an awkward letter from my biological father attempting to explain why he had abandoned me from the beginning. On a dare from a friend, I started calling the Greyhound offices in San Francisco, where the letter told me he worked. Since we shared a name, it wasn't too difficult to track him down. When I got through, his secretary answered. She said he was out, but when she went to take down my name, she realized who I was and gave me the number to his private line. A week later, I called the line.

The first time he answered, I hung up. When I got up the nerve to call back, he answered again, but I didn't say anything. After an interminable pause, he said, "Is this Gino?"

I said, "Yes."

"Well, how are you, bud?" he asked, as if he hadn't been avoiding me and had meant for me to get in touch all along. The conversation couldn't have lasted more than twenty minutes, but it was enough for me to tell him everything—the institutions, bouncing from home to home, the abuse, and how my future was uncertain even now. He didn't or couldn't believe me.

According to him, he and his second wife had offered to take me in, but under the condition that Jackie would not be involved in raising me. She refused. While I was at the Children's Garden, his story went, he was told I already had an adoptive home lined up. This may have been the Nielsons, or it may just have been an excuse on his part. He was convinced this was the best thing for me at the time and testified against Jackie in court, stripping her of her parental rights. He was shocked to hear the reality of my nomadic childhood.

When he got off the phone with me, he called his mother, Nonni, and shared the whole conversation. He warned her that he didn't want their side of the family to have anything more to do with me. It was his way of saving face, I suppose.

Nonni was despondent when she heard what had become of me and passed the news on to her daughter, my aunt Terry, a fiery woman of considerable opinions who was not about to be told what she could or couldn't do when it came to family.

Aunt Terry immediately began the process of tracking me down. Because Jackie's parental rights had been severed and I was still a minor in the eyes of the court, no family members were supposed to be in contact with me, but Terry was relentless. Mrs. White struggled to field the barrage of phone calls. "You're quite the popular fellow!" she told me one day through gritted teeth.

In the end, Aunt Terry found me.

In our first conversation, she told me what had become of my birth mother for the past decade, which wasn't much of a surprise. Jackie was still working in bars. She was hooked on alcohol and cocaine. She was still struggling to get by, spending any money she had, and fighting through the latest in a series of divorces. She talked about me, though, and wondered what had become of me. Aunt Terry said she could put me back in touch if I wanted. I had just moved in with the Dolans and was still reeling from the craziness of the shooting. I could only handle so much at once. I asked to her wait.

I had harbored so much anger at Jackie for giving me up. Ironically, it was Anne who had counseled me and helped me down a path toward forgiveness. Anne was relentless in disparaging anyone who might provide emotional support, but Jackie was so far removed from what it took to be a mother that even Anne didn't feel threatened. Perhaps that realization is what led me to forgive Jackie.

Six months later, after I had met Nonni and a few other members of my biological family through Aunt Terry, I agreed to meet with Jackie. I started by writing her a letter. Terry handed it off and told me Jackie had wept to the point of not being able to stand upon reading it.

When I finally met Jackie again at Terry's house, the solemnity of the moment was somewhat ruined by Terry's tiny dog biting my ankle as I came through the door, but Jackie and I were able to resolve our differences.

I never asked why she hadn't come for me. Why she hadn't turned her life around when her child was on the line. I just don't think she ever had it in her.

For the first time, I was able to let go of the deep fantasy that Jackie would come and "rescue" me, and instead saw her for who she was, someone lost, adrift, and barely able to look after herself. It was a feeling I knew well. I think this is an important rite of passage along the road to adulthood—the moment you see your parents as neither saviors nor villains, but just other flawed human beings. It was a bittersweet reunion after almost ten years, but it provided closure.

After that, we stayed in touch. I called her every other month, wrote her, and saw her from time to time, but she was never really involved in my life. I was fine with that. Sometimes it's better to let the past go.

CHAPTER 16

Unintentional Consequences

My time with the Dolans was one of chaos, growth, setbacks, figuring things out, and stubbornly refusing to figure things out, as teenagers do. Adolescence is difficult. Adolescence for a gay foster kid coming off a rollercoaster of abuse, alcoholism, and attempted murder is something else entirely. It was adolescence on steroids, and the Dolans were not ready for it.

They thought they were, and at another time in my life, they might have been right. They offered me a mix of love, belonging, and structure that might have been enough had I come to them earlier, but they couldn't meet me where I was and accept all the baggage I brought with me.

Joyce and Ken Dolan had already raised three biological children. Brian was in college and Julie was grown and living on her own. The only one living in the house at the time was Christopher, who was two years older than me and a junior in high school. Joyce was kind, but strict, conservative, and strongly opinionated—traits that would clash with my emerging sexuality.

Ken was one of the gentlest men I've ever met. He had a soft-spoken kindness that made me feel understood and at ease right away. I credit him, in large part, for helping me overcome the childhood fear of men that had dogged me since my grandfather's abuse. Many years later, I had the honor of speaking at his funeral. I remember saying it was Ken that taught me how to be a father, or at least the kind of father I wanted to be. Ken was enthusiastic in his support of anything his kids did. Joyce was as well. She just had a different way of expressing it that I only understood later as an adult. For the first time, I felt more connected to a father than a mother. It was an odd feeling.

I went through the motions during the honeymoon period. Although they were very kind to me, I was running on autopilot for the first month I lived with the Dolans. I went through the now-familiar routine of packing and updating addresses in a daze. I wasn't surly or sobbing. I wasn't emotional at all. My old habit of shoving my emotions down and "just getting through it" had returned. It was the adolescent version of staring at my feet. The Dolans did their best to keep their concerns to themselves but didn't know what to do with a blank page.

Inside, I was overwhelmed with conflicting emotions. Anne was still in county jail in Utah awaiting trial. Joe was traveling back and forth. Claudia and Maria were still in school and doing their best to keep their lives on track. I was consumed with worry and guilt over leaving them even just to move across town. After all the times the thought of their well-being had kept me from running away, I felt like I was abandoning them when they needed me most. The elation, guilt, anger over the shooting, feelings of inadequacy, and the black void of starting over with a new family, however kind they tried to be, was more than I could handle. This couldn't go on forever. In the end, even though I am not particularly religious, it was the church that helped break me out of my shell.

I started going to the Dolans' church, which was across town from the one I had attended with Anne and the girls. I was used to the stiff, traditional Catholic church in which I had been an altar boy. The new church, St. Charles, favored plastic chairs over ornate pews and even had altar *girls,* which I considered a shocking scandal at the time. The more liberal atmosphere took some getting used to, but at the Dolans' encouragement, I joined the St. Charles Youth Group.

I showed up to my first youth group meeting stone-faced as usual and sat in the circle. They were discussing a local tragedy. Four teenagers had been killed when their car slammed into a telephone pole at a hundred miles an hour. The youth pastor was doing his best to help us process the enormity of the loss, but the kids around me were openly weeping, holding each other, and shaking with sobs. I didn't say a word but sat alone in my silence. When I got home, Ken and Joyce must have noticed something was off. My mask was cracking. When they asked me how it was, I barked "fine" and fled to my room.

A few minutes later, Joyce tapped on my door and asked if I would come to the living room with her. I thought I was in trouble, but it was an intervention.

"We're concerned about you, Gino," said Ken after I had sat down across from them. "You know you can talk to us. We are here for you."

At first, I sulked, willing myself to hold up the wall against my emotions, but his gentle tone and the genuine look of concern on Joyce's face broke through. A wave of emotion started in the pit of my stomach and grew until it crashed over me. I fell into uncontrollable sobbing. Joyce came to me and wrapped her arms around me in relief.

"There you are," she said, rocking me in her arms. "You are safe. You can let it out."

We spoke into the night. I remember asking how God could finally give me a family and then take it away. I don't remember what they said to me, but I do remember feeling safer than I had felt since I was with Bruni. That night I slept like a rock, and for the first time I could remember, I had an odd sense of peace.

That night I also came to a private realization: I would never live to see the age of thirty. I would never achieve anything significant in my life and I would end up homeless, on drugs, or in jail. These realizations didn't come with fear or anxiety. They just came to me as a fact I accepted as my fate. The years of being made to feel small and insignificant had caught up with me. I had deluded myself for a while, thanks to Anne's unwavering faith in my future, but the truth was I would become a statistic. Something changed in me that night. I started questioning everything because none of it mattered.

I never told the Dolans this, of course, but they never asked. There were a number of wonderful things they did for me that I will never forget, but there was always something missing.

When their daughter, Julie, moved back home with the exciting news that she was pregnant, and then the father of her child proposed to her, the household became a flurry of wedding preparation. The Dolans were sure to make me feel like I was a part of it all. I participated in my first family wedding and witnessed the birth of Julie's beautiful daughter.

They also did some incredible things for just me. I remember coming home from school one day to a waiting phone call from a modeling agent. I had done the few local modeling gigs when I was with Anne, thanks to the shopping mall competition, but this was something new. The agent invited me to join a school in San Francisco. I was thrilled at the prospect, but skeptical about the price. Ken let me know how proud he was, and worked with the Casey Family Program to ensure I could go.

I attended the modeling school every Saturday for a year, learned how to walk, talk, and present myself in the best possible light. Was it cheesy and frivolous? Sure. But for someone trying to find their sense of self and comfort in their own skin, it was as if the entire world had opened up before me. I still remember much of what I was taught to this day.

Through all these positive experiences, though, the feeling that I would amount to nothing, that it was all a waste of time continued to grow. I was burning out, and Joyce didn't see it.

We were both such strong personalities, it was inevitable we would end up butting heads. Pretty soon, the honeymoon was over. Joyce was irritated I was attending the newer, more liberal high school across town that Anne had insisted on. Livermore High was, in her words, "good enough for my kids and should be good enough for you!"

As my grades started to slip in the wake of all the emotional drama with Anne, Joyce gave me an ultimatum halfway through my freshman year: If my grade point average was below a 3.0, I would be moved to Livermore High my sophomore year. It was one of the many things we fought about.

To add to the chaos, I was also beginning to struggle with my sexuality. As lifelong conservative, Catholic Republicans, gay was NOT okay with the Dolans.

I had experienced my first kiss at the age of twelve or thirteen with a neighborhood girl who had beautiful long red hair. We were sitting outside together when she swooped in and planted her lips on mine. Other than the shock, I didn't feel much. No fireworks. No pit in my stomach. No butterflies. Not much of anything. The girl and I hadn't stayed together very long.

In high school, I was athletic, popular, and a model. The girls liked me, and being a teenager anxious to prove my masculinity, sex was always in the picture. I had gone through the motions of sex with girls partly out of a desire to prove my heterosexuality, and partly because I was a walking jumble of intense hormones. Sex with girls didn't hurt and provided a release that even a gay kid needed. But I always walked away feeling guilty and unfulfilled. The butterflies, the pit in your stomach, the fireworks, all of the feelings I had been raised to expect when I was with a girl never happened for me.

I can remember sitting and watching television one night in the family room and a news clip came on with a teaser for the evening news. The story was the 1986 Gay Pride Parade, including brief clips of the event. Joyce curled her lip in disgust at the men holding hands and waving the rainbow flag.

"Those people are sick. That is a sickness!" she said.

To this day, she does not remember saying it.

At the time, it terrified me that such an understanding and loving woman could feel such disgust for people she didn't even know. She would never have knowingly hurt any child, let alone me, but she also never had a problem sharing her opinions. It was an offhand remark. I don't bear her any animosity for it, but it shows how even the smallest moments can have an impact.

Many years later, I was asked to speak to a group of prospective foster parents about what being in foster care was like, and I brought up this experience as an example of how heavy the responsibility of fostering can be. Foster parents are always under an unseen microscope. Kids in their care analyze every word and deed. Even a casual comment can have unintended consequences and affect whether or not a child feels your home is a safe place to be themselves. It wasn't until the early '90s that the Casey Family Program started instituting sensitivity training to help prepare potential foster parents for the possibility that their kids might be gay.

I discovered 900 numbers about the time I was fifteen or sixteen. At the time, porn was just in magazines and there was no internet. Instead, you could call an "adult party line" to hear dirty talk from someone on the other end of the phone—for a minute-by-minute fee. It didn't take me long to discover there were male ones. The first time I called one, I was lying on my bed with my brown clam-shaped phone with the push buttons, holding the disconnect button.

"Hello? Hello? Is anyone here?" said a voice on the line. I was both exhilarated and terrified that I was speaking to another man. I stared at the *Thriller* poster on my ceiling and wasn't able to speak because I was holding my breath. It wasn't long before I called back.

"Hey, hot stuff," said the male voice on the other end.

"Hey," I managed to blurt out.

There was a sense of excitement I had never felt with all the girls I had been with, even more so because it was taboo. I was hooked.

Despite my fear of being found out, my curiosity intensified. I started calling the 900 numbers more often. I just couldn't stop myself. They were my outlet and way of self-discovery. Time after time, I convinced myself these calls were just a temporary fix. Just enough to scratch an itch. I certainly wasn't gay.

Then the Dolans got their $600 phone bill.

It was a *lot* of money in 1986. I don't remember the confrontation, but I'm sure it wasn't pretty. The Casey Family Program ended up paying the bill, but the Dolans made it clear that was beside the point. They felt I had betrayed their trust and gave me a lecture about how this was "not a healthy outlet" for me. Did they realize the numbers were for *male* party lines? Maybe. They didn't bring that up. Maybe they were as afraid to uncork that particular bottle as I was.

At the end of my freshman year, there was no hiding the fact that my grades had started to slide. True to her word, Joyce transferred me to Livermore High for my sophomore year. I was devastated and hated every minute there. I missed all my friends and was back to being an outsider. Using my infallible teenage logic, I sought to get back at her by *really* letting my grades slip. I made the decision to just stop trying. As my sophomore year rolled on, it started looking less and less like I would finish high school. This just reinforced my prediction that I would end up addicted or dead on the street before I reached thirty.

My only respite from the pointless doldrums of school were my friends in the youth group. That's where I met Erica, a tall, very outgoing girl with a waterfall of honey-blond hair. She was a year ahead of me at Livermore High and lived just around the corner. Erica came from a broken home, and we commiserated over our familial struggles. She was the first person I ever talked to about how my grandfather abused me. She would become one of my strongest friends and supporters throughout the following years.

About two-thirds of the way through my sophomore year, the Dolans hit the wall with me. The last straw was another $600+ phone bill (the third or fourth one).

I came home from a youth group retreat and was told I would be moving. They weren't sure where yet, but I would be told in a few days.

Here we go again.

I had experienced yet another change in social worker during my stay with them as well. Mrs. White retired not long after I moved in. When Anne had gotten back from jail, I had kept in contact with her regularly. When I told her about how much I had enjoyed wilderness survival camp a year or two earlier, she suggested I ask if Bruce, the counselor I had gotten along with so well, wanted to step in as my social worker. She pointed out I had never had a male social worker. I had seen Bruce off and on since the wilderness camp, and we had always gotten along. I thought it would be a great fit. I asked if he'd be willing to work with me, and he agreed.

The Dolans never trusted him because he had smoked pot in college and claimed it had been "no big deal." Joyce was not amused, nor would I have been as an adult if it was someone responsible for one of my kids, but he was good to me, at least at first. During a conversation with him at a Casey Family Program event about a year before he became my social worker, I asked him about Chris, a cute boy from the camp that I had bonded with (and had a secret crush on). Bruce just grimaced and said, "We lost him to the gay underworld," with a tone of disgust. I didn't think much of it at the time, except that it was an odd reaction, but his attitude toward my sexuality would become a major hurdle in the years to come.

Around the end of my time with the Dolans, his attitude toward me changed almost overnight. He became manipulative, bureaucratic, and petty—the opposite of Kathee and Mrs. White. It was as if someone had flipped a switch. I still believe the reason for this was his homophobia. He must have seen the report on the 900 numbers and figured out which ones I had been calling. Two days later, he called me to tell me where I would be moving: back in with Anne.

"What?" I said into the phone.

He seemed annoyed. "It's just temporary until we can find something more suitable."

I was confused. If they saw Anne as an acceptable guardian, why had they taken me away in the first place?

She had been released from jail after only six months. During her trial, Gladys had told the judge the shooting was accidental, and Anne should be given leniency. As a result, she had been released from jail, put on probation, and could no longer be a teacher. Apparently being a foster parent was still just fine, though. She had come home to Livermore to try and pick up the pieces, sell her house, and move back East. How on Earth Bruce thought that house was a good place to put me, even temporarily, is still a mystery. But one morning, we packed up my stuff yet again and made the drive across town.

Anne was a mess. Now there was no hiding her mental illness. Her drinking was out of control, and she rarely left the house. Claudia was still there too. She stayed with Anne until she got married several years later, but in those days, she was just trying to get through high school and graduate. I, on the other hand, was on the brink of dropping out. I had achieved my goal of failing every single class my sophomore year.

Anne had already kicked Maria out, and she was living with her boyfriend somewhere. Needless to say, things were tense. The stress of uncertainty was unbearable. Not knowing where I was going, when I was going, or who I was to live with weighed on me until I was so broken and scared that I struggled to even function day to day.

One night, I was so stressed that I remember being in tears, but then realized I was across town in a Safeway parking lot with no idea how I got there. Four hours had passed. I was not drunk or high. I was just so full of anxiety that I needed to move forward in any way I could. The blackout terrified me. I had suffered a lot throughout my childhood, but I had always been able to get through it. This was something new. It was inside me, and I wasn't sure I could get past it.

Thankfully, I had Erica to help me. Laughter is a powerful elixir, and with Erica I could laugh with wild abandon and no judgement. Our friendship was cemented into a lifelong bond in those few short months.

I stayed with Anne and Claudia until I completed my sophomore year. I didn't hear a word from Bruce the whole time I was there. He just left me with a known felon for almost two months. About mid-May, he called me. He told me once the school year had finished, I would be moving in with the Roberts.

CHAPTER 17

Beating the System

I said nothing, but tears were streaming down my face. I had a sense I would end up with the Roberts, but I kept trying to talk myself out of it. Now it was reality. In a rare movement of sober clarity, Anne offered to take me to meet with them again. This time Wava Roberts didn't even bother with the pretense. It was explained to me that I would not be allowed to use the phone without permission and the phone in the kitchen would be locked. I was shown the room I would be sharing. I was shocked that the polyester blue bedspread was identical to the ones at the Dependent Unit. Even the mattress was covered in plastic.

When Anne and I left the Roberts' Home for Children, she looked at me with such sadness I felt compelled to comfort her. She didn't say much, but I knew she felt she had failed me. I also knew she was far too fragile to take my issues on. I said, "It'll be okay. I'll be eighteen next summer and can do what I want. I can do it for a year."

As unhappy as I was to be moving in with the Roberts, at least I was back on the other side of town and could return to Granada High School instead of Livermore High. I did my best to follow the house rules but was in a hole of distrust from day one because I had thrown them over for the Dolans two years before. The feeling was mutual. The Roberts were a means to an end in my mind. I kept my distance and reminded myself I would be out in a year.

The Roberts were used to taking in severely troubled kids and very much lived by the consistency-over-care model. They were out of touch with "normal" kids and handled every issue with regimented policies—not abusive but controlling. Ironically, this meant that after all the situations in which I had been too difficult for my would-be parent figures, I now found myself to be too well-adjusted to tolerate their ridiculous rules about everything. I remember they grounded me once because I vacuumed up my cat's litter and they said I was trying to ruin the vacuum cleaner. When I pushed back even a little, I was grounded for weeks. It didn't take long to learn to keep my mouth shut and fight back in subtler ways.

For my seventeenth birthday, Wava announced that she would allow me to have a pool party.

"Really? That sounds great!" I said.

"Of course, we expect it won't be any more than ten friends. We'd like it to be under four hours, and not at night." She listed off the conditions on her fingers.

At this point, being back at Granada, I had a lot of friends. I was turning seventeen, not seven, but I was polite.

"Yeah. I'll think about it," I said.

Billy was one of my best buddies at the time. Like most of my friends, I had met him through youth group at the church.

I was over at his house not long after the birthday party conversation. His mom, Maria, was teaching me how to heat up tortillas on a gas burner. As we worked, Billy dropped the subject of my birthday into the conversation.

"They said he can only have, like, ten kids!" he told her.

"What is he, seven?" she asked. Maria was a local school bus driver and had no tolerance for nonsense.

"That's what I was thinking," I chimed in. "I know twenty kids from youth group alone!"

Maria flipped a tortilla onto a plate like a judge banging a gavel.

"You'll have it here," she said, settling the matter without even looking up from her cooking. "I'll call them," she said. "I got this."

Billy gave me the thumbs-up.

Wava was livid that I had asked to have my birthday party somewhere else. I sat there stone-faced on the plastic couch as she lectured me.

"Look," I said. "Let's not pretend like you like me or I like you. I know what you think of me, and I am okay with that because I am only here out of necessity."

She feigned shock well, or maybe she actually was shocked that I had called her out.

"What? Why would you say that? Mr. Roberts and I *love* you," she pleaded.

"If that's true, then you should understand my friends are all I have. Ten people?" I asked. I pulled a crumpled piece of binder paper out of my pocket. Billy and I had made up a guest list. It was roughly fifty kids…and their parents. It would be less than a mile away and the Roberts were invited to come if they wanted.

Checkmate.

The Roberts didn't come, and I was fine with that. It was an incredible party. I was in heaven. It felt like home.

After the birthday party, I remember making the conscious decision that I needed to start turning my schoolwork around again, if not for my future, then at least to grease the wheels with the Roberts. I knew as long as I was getting good grades and following their ridiculous rules, they would leave me alone. If I was going to die young, I might as well do everything I could to have a good time before the end.

Going into my junior year, I was determined to apply myself to my schoolwork. I still wasn't sure how I would be able to graduate since I had failed my entire sophomore curriculum except driver's ed.

"I think you're just too far behind to graduate next year," Wava would say with a sigh that oozed superior disappointment.

Even my guidance counselor didn't think I could do it, but the Roberts required I come straight home from school. I would just avoid them by going straight to my room and doing my homework. My grades shot up. I went from all Fs to straight As in one semester. As my grades improved, so did my confidence. I was on a better track, but graduation was still a long way off. Senioritis would not be an option the following year.

The Roberts set a weekend curfew of ten o'clock. I only missed it once. I had been to visit Jackie, and my bus was late getting in. When I walked in the door, it was ten thirty. I apologized for being late, and Mr. Roberts snapped at me that I smelled like alcohol.

"I've been on a Greyhound bus for eight hours," I said. He said nothing, but I could tell he was cataloguing the incident as a piece of ammunition to be used against me later.

The following day, I called my doctor from a payphone and asked if he would give me a blood test. I told him my foster parents had accused me of smelling like alcohol and I was worried they would try to stop me from seeing my birth mother by saying she allowed me to drink. The doctor instructed me to come down right away. It was an hour's walk each way and I didn't have a car, but it was worth it to ensure the Roberts didn't have anything on me.

When I came home from school the following Friday, the Roberts had called for reinforcements. Bruce was there.

We all sat in the plastic-lined living room. Mrs. Roberts put on her usual show, and even went so far as the traditional baking of cookies that said, "*See what caring parents we are.*"

Bruce didn't smile as he shoved a piece of paper in my direction.

"What is this?" he demanded. It was the results of the blood test.

"Oh good, they came," I said, looking Mr. Roberts dead in the eye. "Now you'll believe me when I said I was not drinking."

"Gino—you can't just go off and get a blood test without telling anyone," Bruce said. "We got a surprise bill for over $200."

I shrugged. "I don't know what to tell you, Bruce, but I am not willing to risk any of you telling me I can't see my mother. Next time maybe you can give me the benefit of the doubt and not make comments that make me feel threatened. I can't tell you I won't do it again. Are we done here? I have homework."

I shoved the test results back at Bruce and marched up to my room, smiling to myself. I had learned to play the long game.

In a way, as much as it seemed a low point, my stay with the Roberts might have been just what I needed. They represented everything I hated about the institutional side of foster care: the "processing plant" mentality typified by a lack of trust and viewing children as objects to be managed and churned through for profit. Pushing back against them was pushing back against the system itself. I was able to use all the skills I had learned in the school of hard knocks from all the families I had lived with. I was smarter, stronger, and more resourceful than before. I was also armed with the unshaking belief that I only had a few years to live. I had nothing to lose. I never did anything bad while I was with the Roberts. Never acted out or disobeyed, but I learned how to play the game, and I played it well.

After the drug test, they became even more controlling. They tried to limit my attendance to youth group. I reached out to Bruce, and, as usual, he sided with the Roberts. I went over his head. I called the Casey Family Program's office and spoke to his supervisor, Carmen. She invited me to the office, and Bruce picked me up a week later. The drive was awkward at best.

When we sat down with Carmen, she slid a piece of paper across the table to me. "Have you ever seen this?" she asked. It was the Foster Care Bill of Rights, which The Casey Family Program helped draft and is now law. The second right on the list stated that I was to be free to attend religious service of any kind at any time, without restriction.

I slid the paper to Bruce and snapped, "What the fuck? You knew about this? Why am I not surprised?"

I asked Carmen for a copy before we left. I grinned and hummed to myself on the drive home as Bruce seethed in the driver's seat. As I was getting out of the car, I said, "So we are clear, neither you nor the Roberts can ever tell me I can't go to my youth group again."

When I walked into the house, Mr. and Mrs. Roberts were watching TV. I handed them the copy of the bill of rights Carmen had given me, smiled, and went to my room. They never said another word about it when I left for anything related to church.

With my newfound sense of control, I sailed through the first semester of my junior year. The dance with the Roberts continued on a daily basis, but I managed to keep them at arm's length.

In January of 1988, I went to a church retreat through the youth group called SEARCH, which was for high school upper classmen and college students.

On the very first day of the retreat, a tall, freckled girl jogged up to me with a grace that belied her six-foot frame. She flashed a dazzling smile, and I had the sense I'd seen her somewhere before.

"You probably don't remember me," she said. "I was at your birthday party last year at Billy's house. Becky..."

She extended a hand, and I took it.

"I'm Gino."

She grinned. "I know, silly."

We immediately hit it off and hardly left each other's side for the entire weekend of the retreat. We opened up and shared the stories of our childhoods. As one of the assignments, we were supposed to write someone a letter. She wrote one to me. I still have it somewhere.

When the retreat was over, she went back to college, and we started a long-distance friendship. She was a college freshman, and I was a high school junior, but we were only a year apart in age. She would call me when she wasn't in class or at volleyball practice. When she was home on the weekends, we would go on little adventures. We drove to the coast or to visit my birth mother and started dating soon after. She had never had a boyfriend and I was still struggling with my own sexuality, but I did love her. The Roberts liked her too, which was helpful. She saw right through them, though, which made her all the more appealing to me.

About a month after we started officially dating, we were on the way out for one of our weekend road trips.

"Hey," she said. "Do you mind if we stop by my parents' house for a couple minutes, so I can run in. I forgot a few things."

"Umm…okay." I gave myself a cursory check in the mirror. Meeting the parents is always a big deal, but Becky was an only child and the apple of their eyes. I was sure they thought I wasn't good enough for her, and deep down, I agreed. I was desperate to make a good impression.

Frank, Becky's father, was in the driveway when we pulled up. He stopped washing his car long enough to give us a friendly wave. Becky ushered me through a gate and around to the backyard where her mom was lying on a lounge chair in a yellow bikini and holding a large foil-covered sun reflector at her chest. She gave us little more than a glance before waving me over to the chair beside her. She had a warm, open face and wore large glasses like Dustin Hoffman in *Tootsie*. I liked her immediately.

"You must be Gino," she said. "I've heard a lot about you. I'm Judy."

The two of us sat in the backyard and talked for about half an hour as Becky gathered her stuff. By the time she was ready to leave, I knew these people were kind and safe. As we said our goodbyes, Frank said, "Come by anytime! Even if Becky is away at school, you can come by."

As my junior year drew to a close, not having a car was becoming a real hassle. I had been walking to school, but April and May can be very rainy in our area of Northern California, and it was often coming down in sheets. Of course, the Roberts were never going to give me a ride. I often juggled cars with Becky while she was off at college during the week. Soon, even this arrangement became a challenge. Becky happened to have some money from an inheritance sitting in a savings account. It wasn't long before she and her parents hatched a plan to get me my own car.

They found a 1982 Mercury Capri for $2,000 and gave me a loan from Becky's inheritance to buy it. It was just what I needed to get me through the end of school and give me some independence. I promised I would pay them back with interest, and a few years later, I did. There was a bigger problem, though.

Judy knew the Roberts would not be happy with loosening my leash even a little. She gave Wava a call and laid out her reasoning. She asked permission before buying the car and let her know the details of the purchase, insurance, and financing. After a lot of back and forth, she got Wava to agree and give permission for the car. All of this happened without my knowledge because the car was meant to be a surprise.

It certainly was a surprise. When the car arrived, Wava had a meltdown. I came home from school, and she sat me down in the living room and started shouting at me. She told me I was grounded and threatened to kick me out of the house. I just sat there thunderstruck. I had no idea what was going on. By this time, I knew the car was coming, but I also knew she had cleared it. When she had finished shouting, she sent me to my room and told me I was grounded.

The following morning, I was headed out the door to school, when she caught me and told me I was grounded and not allowed to leave the house. I just laughed.

"I'm going to school," I said. "It's Friday."

"If you don't get back in here," she said, "I'm going to call the cops and report you as a runaway!"

I shrugged. "Go ahead. They'll find me at school, and when school's done, I'll be on my way back here." I walked out the door.

She never called the cops. I went to school and went straight to my room when I came home. While at school, I told some of the kids what was going on, and it didn't take long for word to get out.

The next day, someone came to the front door with a book. It was one of Judy's neighbors. She told Wava her daughter had a computer class with me and had borrowed one of the books I needed. She handed Wava the book. It was *Macintosh for Dummies*. Of course, there was no computer class. It was 1988. Computers weren't even a common household item yet, but Wava didn't catch on. She had no idea what classes I was taking in school. She came up and tossed the book into my room.

"Here's the book you loaned that girl," she said, closing the door after her.

I was confused at first and then I realized something must be up. I grabbed the book and pored over it to see if anything was highlighted or if there was some sort of code. I couldn't find anything. After nearly twenty minutes of searching, I laid it out flat on my desk and there, right against the spine, was a line of text in Judy's handwriting. Every page contained a line of the letter. The gist was encouragement to stay strong and an assurance that "we're working to get you out."

The ridiculousness of it made me laugh out loud. It was like I was in some sort of Siberian gulag with notes being smuggled to me by the underground…in a copy of *Macintosh for Dummies*. Judy always had a way of being supportive and encouraging while finding the quirky humor in any situation.

On Monday, I went back to school and Bruce showed up on campus. I could tell by his demeanor he was furious. My time in the system was coming to an end, and I had found people who supported and cared for me. He could sense his control over me was tenuous at best, as could the Roberts.

He pulled me out of class and marched me over to the conference room in the office building. By this time, I was smart enough to know that witnesses were everything. The community offered more than just support. They offered accountability. I followed him into the room but was careful to leave the door open a bit. The ladies who worked in the school office, all of whom knew and liked me, could hear every word of our conversation.

Bruce fumed. "Congratulations," he said. "You're about to be emancipated from the Casey Family Program." This meant they would no longer pay for anything, including college. He was threatening to cut me off without a cent and make me homeless. But of course, social workers don't get to make those decisions, and I knew it.

I just stared at him with a blank expression. "Why?" I asked. "What did I do that was so bad that I would be emancipated?"

He continued to rant, getting more and more nonsensical as he went on. Every time he paused for breath, I just asked again, "What. Did. I. Do?" He never could answer.

Finally, he blurted out, "You'll be emancipated immediately unless you agree never to see Frank, Judy, or Becky again!"

I just asked him again what I had done, and he stormed out.

As I left the conference room, one of the office ladies asked if I was okay and if I needed a place to stay.

"I don't think so," I said. "I'll let you know, but I think it'll work out."

Then I called Judy. "Come live with us" was the first thing she said. I started making arrangements for my final move while in foster care.

I went to stay with Frank and Judy for the night and then recruited a friend for the move. We pulled up at the Roberts' Home for Children to find all my worldly possessions out on the front lawn, including the cat, which they had put in a moving box and taped it shut.

I suppose I shouldn't have been shocked by this, but I was. After all, the Roberts had been proclaiming over and over again about how much they *loved* me. But now that I was on my way out, the veil had fallen. They wanted nothing to do with me. I was a commodity and always had been. Of course,

I had known this from the very beginning, but perhaps the part of me that had always wanted to belong had been taken in by their facade.

I didn't cry as we packed the cars. In fact, I was more convinced than ever I had made the right choice.

Every six months or so during my entire tenure in foster care there had been a hearing to check in and assess my well-being. I had never been to one before. I hadn't even known they were going on for most of my childhood. I can't begin to imagine what they discussed during the time when I was being shuttled from one abusive home to another. Probably not much. The system was so overburdened that cases like mine were rushed through and given little more than a perfunctory glance before being stamped and passed off for another half year.

Now I was old enough to have a say in my own fate. Judy and I planned for me to attend the next hearing. Judy insisted on hiring a minor's rights attorney. There was a lot at stake. If Bruce and the Roberts had their way, I would be kicked out of the Casey Family Program and lose financial support for my education, healthcare, and just about everything else.

When the appointed day came, I showed up at court with Judy, Frank, and the attorney. Bruce and the Roberts were there too, but not for long. Before the hearing started, the attorney approached the bench and spoke to the judge. The judge then beckoned me over and spoke to me in a low tone.

"This is your hearing, and it is for your benefit. Is there anyone here who you don't wish to be in attendance?"

I nodded and said I would like the Roberts not to be there. The judge nodded back and sent us back to our table before asking the Roberts to leave the courtroom. It was a small moment, but it felt huge. The system was starting to work in my favor, and I was figuring out how to use it.

Next came the documented testimony of the ladies in the school office who had overheard Bruce's talk of emancipation, which he had no power to do and no right to threaten. From there on, anything he had to say against me fell apart like a sandcastle at high tide. I was allowed to move in with Frank and Judy. Although I was no longer to be considered an active member of the Casey Family Program. However, after I graduated from high school, I was still considered an alumnus. This status allowed me to maintain most of my benefits and would continue to support me into young adulthood. It was still up to me to get through high school on my own without a social worker or help from the Casey Family Program, but it was the best of both worlds: liberation and support. It was a major win!

CHAPTER 18

Love & Acceptance

Moving in with Frank and Judy (we didn't start calling her "Juju" until the name was babbled into existence by my baby niece over a decade later) was the most natural thing ever. There was no honeymoon period because it just felt *real* from the beginning. That's not to say there was never conflict, but Judy made it clear in every moment and every word that she would never give up on me. She recognized what had happened to me was wrong and accepted the challenges that came with it. She would say over and over, "I know it's hard to trust, but I'm never going to leave you." That's all it took. That and just listening to what I needed. She knew when I was upset and never pushed me to hide or cover it up for her benefit. She just met me where I was and stayed there with me.

I'm not going to lie; she also spoiled me rotten. She was always free with money and would buy me anything I wanted. I remember going clothes shopping with her and being in the dressing room while she tossed item after item over the door. "Try this one," she'd say, or, "What do you think about this?"

In the end, I would walk out with bags of clothes for school or summer. It was a gesture of limitless acceptance that was about so much more than just clothes. It was about the effort. Knowing someone is running around a store finding things in your size, not because they have to, but because they value you as a person, speaks volumes.

Of course, I did get into a little trouble now and again doing the normal stupid teenage boy things, but I never acted out or butted heads with Frank and Judy as I had with past foster parents. Perhaps I didn't feel the need to test the relationship because I knew it was real.

When I moved in, I also met Mary, who would become like a sister to me. Mary's mom had been best friends with Judy and had died of breast cancer when Mary was seventeen. Frank and Judy had agreed to take Mary in. She had come to live with them six months before I did. She was small—some might say mousy—with kind, thoughtful eyes, and a quiet, fierce intelligence that hid a hint of mischief.

Mary had been very close to her biological mother. Although she was grateful to Judy for taking her in, she didn't want to think of her as her mother. "There's no rule that says you can only have one. Judy doesn't replace your mother," I said. "She's just a second mother."

Senior year of high school was crazy and magical. I was still recovering from my disastrous sophomore year. Frank and Judy both helped me study with flashcards and tutoring whenever they could. They were committed to helping me succeed. With their help, I managed to make up my entire sophomore year of high school while a senior, which was a minor miracle. I was in day school, night school, had a part-time job as part of a work-study program (to earn graduation credit), was a class officer, and still managed to have an amazing senior year. Judy used to leave work, stop at a fast-food joint, and swing by my night school class to feed us all. It was a struggle, but by the end of senior year, it was clear I would be graduating in June with the rest of my friends in the class of 1989.

My social life also flourished during this time. It has always come as a surprise to me how some people don't maintain their high school relationships or even hated high school. The friendships I made in my youth group and in school have endured throughout my adult life. I became the glue of my friend group and the person in charge of organizing all our reunions. We lived on a cul-de-sac, and my room was a converted two-car garage, so it was massive. This enabled me to have friends over all the time, and Judy always let me have my space to be social. School had always been my safe place, but now I also had a home I didn't feel ashamed of.

Oftentimes we would have drunken parties in my garage "room," and friends would end up reeling on the couch while Judy held the "silver bowl of shame" for them to throw up in. She was always there but never hovered, and her faith never wavered.

She was also quite prim. Not conservative as such, but she had a strong sense of propriety. One of the upsides to living in the converted garage was that there was a big refrigerator in my room. One night while I was trying to sleep, she kept coming in to reach into the fridge for her box of cheap Franzia wine. Each time she came in, she was a little tipsier and less subtle about it. She had a favorite nightgown that was in the popular style of a shortened muumuu and barely covered the essentials. The final time she came in, she had to lean way over and tip the box forward. I got a lot more of an eyeful than I wanted or had bargained for. The next day I mentioned she might want to think about wearing a longer nightgown or else putting on some underwear if she was going to keep her wine on such a low shelf in the fridge. She turned the brightest shade of red I've ever seen. She was mortified. It wasn't until much later that we were able to laugh about it.

Despite all the kindness and good times, there was still a part of me that doubted it would last. I had been disappointed too many times before and I had a secret. One I feared would come out someday and make me unacceptable, even to Judy. Somewhere in the back of my mind, I still had the absolute certainty that I would be homeless or dead by my thirtieth birthday. Throughout high school, whenever I saw a homeless person, I felt an unspoken kinship. Part of it had to do with my background, but I was coming to realize there was something about me that just didn't fit the prescribed path to success laid out by our small, conservative, religious community.

During the first few months after I moved in with Frank and Judy, Becky and I inevitably broke up, which created quite a bit of tension. I wouldn't allow myself to see exactly how much until much later. Things went smoothly enough during the school year, but the summer we were both at home was uncomfortable, to say the least.

Frank had never been a great husband to Judy, to be honest, but he lavished attention on Becky and tolerated my hijinks with patience. Looking back on that time, I'm glad Becky had him to turn to. She had grown up with quite a bit of privilege. She was an athletic star, good student, and the apple of her parents' eyes. Within the space of a couple years, she went from being an only child to one of three. I went from being her ex-boyfriend to being her brother and was doted on by her mother. It was a difficult adjustment, and the more Judy accepted me into the family, the more Becky resented me and her mother for it.

I've always been a people pleaser, though, and I wanted Becky to like me, so I avoided this conflict. We never spoke much about it, but it was always simmering under the surface. When my secret came to light, however, my relationship to both Juju and Becky would change forever.

During my senior year, one of my many activities was managing a small frozen yogurt shop part time. The shop was in the Payless shopping center across the street from the high school. Frozen yogurt was a popular fad in the 1980s, and these little shops were everywhere. This one was called "My Hearts Delight Yogurt."

One day, a guy with a mop of curly hair and a lean, romance-novel body stuffed into tight 501s strolled into the shop and flashed me a smile.

"Can I get a chocolate with sprinkles?"

"Sure," I said, making sure my voice didn't crack.

"I've seen you here a lot," he said. "I work at the Payless across the way. Name's Kevin."

We started talking, and every time he came into the shop, I tried not to think about how well he filled out those jeans.

One slow Friday night, he asked me if I wanted to hang out after I closed up.

"I…I guess so," I said. "What did you have in mind?"

"I dunno. There's not much to do around here. We can just chat in my car for a while, though. We can get some beer."

At eighteen, I was impressed. His ability to buy beer made him just that much more attractive. We sat in his car, drank, and talked. After an hour or so, my nerves were calmer, and we exchanged phone numbers before parting ways. I still thought he was cute, but my nervousness had disappeared.

Kevin started coming into the shop a lot more often after that and we became buddies. One afternoon he called me and asked me if I wanted to come over to his house and hang out. He lived with his parents in Tracy, which is about twenty minutes east of Livermore. I still had a little crush on him, but I didn't want to make waves, so I kept it to myself. I drove down to his house, and we hung out in his room.

I remember the smell of his room as being very masculine. We were sitting on the edge of his bed, and he was showing me his album collection. He was talking about the artwork on the cover for *Loverboy*. As he handed the album to me, he leaned into me as that red-haired neighbor girl had done all those years before. Before I knew it, he was kissing me. I pulled back from him in a panic.

"I'm sorry!" he said. "I thought…I thought…I mean…I thought you were into me! I'm so sorry!" He was trying desperately to backpedal.

But by then, all the feelings I had always been told should happen when I was with a girl hit me at once. My knees were weak, my stomach was doing flip-flops, my head was spinning, and I saw stars. All I wanted was more! As Kevin was stumbling over his words and trying to repair what he thought would be the end of our friendship, I grabbed him, pulled him to me, and kissed him back. We made out on his bed for what seemed like hours. He was gracious and respectful of my lack of experience. A few days after our first kiss, Kevin and I had oral sex and there was no more denying it; I knew I was gay.

A week later, I sat through graduation day in a fog. To this day, most of my last week of high school is a blur, but I do remember sitting in my chair during the ceremony thinking, "What the fuck am I going to do now?" I lived in terror that Frank and Judy would find out I was gay. They would kick me to the curb, and who would blame them? It wouldn't be long now before I would lose my home and the family it had taken me so long to find.

I felt so conflicted and ashamed that I didn't think I could face grad night. My best friend, Erica, was living in San Diego at this point, so I thought maybe I could drive down and spend some time with her instead. Judy handed me her credit card and told me to have a great time because I deserved it after all my hard work senior year.

I don't know if I was testing the relationship, if I thought that I was about to be homeless, so I might as well have one last fling, or if I wasn't thinking at all like a normal high-school boy, but Erica and I ended up racking up $5,000 in credit card debt in a few short days. We went to every amusement park, stayed in the fanciest hotels, and ate at the best restaurants. It was an amazing, stupid vacation.

When Judy heard about the trip and saw the bill, she didn't bat an eye. "Well," she said, "I guess that will just be your graduation present from us then." And that was that. When Frank heard about the trip and guessed at what it must have cost, he was shocked. She told him Erica's mom had paid for it as a graduation gift and I didn't let on. At graduation, Frank saw Erica's mom and thanked her profusely for her generosity. She was wise enough not to let on either.

Kevin and I dated on and off that summer on the sly. He told me about a new gay bar that was closer to home in the town of Walnut Creek called Just Rewards, or J.R.'s for short. He had taken me to a gay bar in San Francisco for my nineteenth birthday (with the help of a fake ID), but I had never been to one on my own. Finally, unable to quench my curiosity, I called J.R.'s and a very effeminate-sounding guy answered. I asked him for directions, and he chirped them to me with glee.

"Be sure to say hi when you get here! You sound handsome!"

"Um, okay, sure…" I mumbled.

At nineteen and scared shitless, I walked into a gay bar on my own for the very first time. It was a weeknight, so the bar wasn't very busy. There was no one at the door checking IDs. As I entered the darkened room, I saw a small stage in the very front. There were about twenty tables spread out in front of the stage. As I continued past the chairs, I noticed some of the tables had been pushed together and a group of guys sitting at this larger table started catcalling and whistling at me as I walked by. I shot back a nervous smile and headed to the bar. The well-worn counter formed a large triangle with a window onto the empty dance floor. Janet Jackson's "Control" thumped and popped in the background.

Behind the bar, a man in his late thirties with a slight frame, curly dark hair, and a little bit of a belly bounced in time to the music as he cleaned. He smiled when he saw me approach.

"What can I get ya, handsome!?"

"Um…a beer, I guess," I said.

His head flipped around. "Did you call me about an hour and a half ago and ask for directions?"

"Ya. That was me," I mumbled.

"You ARE as handsome as you sounded on the phone!"

"Thank you," I said, my face feeling flush.

"Come on, let me introduce you to the boys." He slid from behind the bar with my beer in one hand, grabbed me with the other, and dragged me over to the table of hecklers. One by one he introduced me to everyone. I got to know them all, but one in particular couldn't take his hands off of me and I was all too willing to receive the attention. Eventually, he managed to talk me into going out to his car. There isn't a lot you can do in a car, but there was enough. From then on, though, I became a regular at J.R.'s. I met quite a few people and slept with most of them.

About two months after I started going to J.R.'s, the bomb dropped. Judy came to me one afternoon and said, "There was a big article about that bar you said you like to go to, J.R.'s, in the *San Francisco Chronicle*. It said it was a gay bar. Why are you going to a gay bar? Are you gay?" The words bounced around my head. My mind raced for excuses as I panicked behind what I hoped was a neutral mask.

"NO!" I yelled. "I only go there because they don't question my fake ID. There are a lot of straight people that go there!" Judy sensed she shouldn't push the issue. "Oh. Okay, honey. That makes sense," was all she said, but I knew the truth would come out sooner or later.

The more time I spent at J.R.'s, the stronger my desire became to come out as gay. I had started junior college but was still exhausted and burned out from my final push to graduate high school. I had a lame job making $5 an hour and was lacking the life skills needed for independence. I was convinced Frank and Judy would kick me out if they found out, but lying about who I was began to weigh on me.

Bruce had made it very clear to me that the Casey Family Program didn't support gay kids. (He was lying, of course, but I didn't find that out until several years later.) I had already come out to Erica, but Judy was a wild card whom I had come to depend on. Coming out to her was one of the hardest things I have ever done.

It was a Friday night, and I was in my room alone. Judy got home from work and asked me what my plans were for the night. "Nothing," I said. "I'm tired and I'm just going to stay home." She knew me well enough to know something wasn't right. About an hour later, she edged back into my room holding a glass of wine, plopped herself on the couch that sat next to my bed, and said, "So…I'm a little worried about you. Are you okay?"

"I'm okay. I just have a lot on my mind, that's all."

"Do you want to talk about it?"

I swallowed hard. "Yeah, but I don't know how to say it."

She looked puzzled. "Is anyone pregnant, dead, dying, hurt, sick, or in danger? Serious question."

"No, no, nothing like that," I said.

"Then whatever it is can't be that bad." Judy always tried to be upbeat and positive, but I knew there was always a moment when it went south with an adopted family. I just hadn't been able to pinpoint that moment so exactly before. I was sure this was going to be it—the beginning of a slide that would end with me dead on the sidewalk.

"I can't say it," I said, bursting into tears. Judy looked terrified.

"Gino…Look, I know it's hard for you to believe after everything you have been through, but we are going to be together for a long, long time. There is nothing you can say that will make me stop loving you."

"I'm scared you will kick me out," I said, shuddering with tears.

I remember her shoulders dropping and the look of fear leaving her face. "Is this about the bar in Walnut Creek you've been going to?" she asked. I nodded. "The gay bar?" she said sheepishly.

"Yeah," I said, staring at my feet as if I were five again. "I think…I think…I think I might…" I stopped. I couldn't say the words. They would not come out of my mouth.

"Okay, now the last time we talked about this you got really mad at me, so if you promise not to get mad at me, I'm going to ask you a question, okay?" Judy was treading very lightly. Between my tears and trembling, I could barely see her.

"Okay."

"Are you trying to tell me that you think you might be gay?"

And there it was. Spoken out loud and echoing in my head. My deepest, darkest, most terrifying secret had just come to light.

"I'm so sorry," I blurted out.

"Sorry for what?" Judy asked.

"Because you and Frank have done so much for me, and I don't deserve it! I'm not worth it!"

It was her turn to be angry. She straightened her spine, uncrossed her legs, and leaned closer.

"Listen, I honestly don't know what to say to you to make you believe what you just said is complete garbage. I don't care if you are gay, if you are straight, if you're Black, if you are white, or purple! I love you and that will never change. Not ever. Do you hear me? You are a son to me. I wish I had the words to tell you that would make you understand. There is nothing wrong with you." She clung to my hand as she spoke, and her eyes were steady. I had never heard her speak with such determination. "I want to make a suggestion to you. I think you should go to see my therapist. I don't want you to see her because there is something wrong with you, but because I don't know what to say to you that will make you understand you are totally okay."

I was stunned. In complete shock. "You don't hate me?"

"God no! Never!" She got up from the couch and asked if she could give me a hug. I was sobbing again as she wrapped her loving arms around me. A lifetime of shame and fear came pouring out of me.

"You are going to be okay, honey! I promise, and I will be there with you always."

I had lived with the family for a year, but this was the moment Judy became my mother and I became her son. I had never felt that kind of unconditional love before from anyone other than Bruni. I started seeing the therapist not long thereafter. I had been going to psychologists and psychiatrists since I was four years old, but this was the first time I saw any value in it. In the long run, it would set me up to be conscious of my mental health and give me a willingness to take steps to care for my emotional well-being.

CHAPTER 19

Mistakes Made & Tough Choices

After high school, my life became a series of aimless wanderings. The system and my experiences with my various foster and adoptive families had left me ill-prepared for the responsibilities of adult life. I didn't know how to manage money, hold a job, or change a tire. I was exhausted from the roller coaster of my high school years, and after a dismal attempt at junior college, I moved down to Santa Barbara with a group of my school friends, only to move back home a few months later when Frank called to tell me he was leaving Judy.

I asked him if he was leaving because he had someone else. He assured me that there was no one else, but there had been problems in their marriage for a long time. I took him at his word, but later I found out that he had been having an affair with one of Judy's friends from college. I lost all respect for him. He didn't just leave Judy, he left me and Mary too. Becky, possibly still bitter about being ousted from her only-child status by her ex-boyfriend, turned her back on her mother to side with Frank, causing a rift that would never truly heal between us.

Even though he treated Judy terribly, in my opinion, he did make sure all the money they received from the foster program went to my care. He placed each check in an account for me to use whenever I needed money for car repairs or other major expenses. Many years later, when I had the chance at a family event, I made a point of thanking him for what he did for me. This act of compassion had a profound effect on my later success. I am proud I was able to do the same for my own adopted kids later in life.

Judy was devastated by the divorce. After what had happened with Anne, I was terrified she might hurt herself. I could barely take care of myself and had no idea how to be a support system for her. I was having anxiety attacks on a regular basis.

I jumped from one meaningless sexual encounter to the next. I still consider it something of a miracle that I never got HIV or other STDs, as the epidemic was still far from under control. I was still seeing the therapist Judy recommended after I came out to her and was getting some value out of it, but not enough to counter my feeling of being rudderless. The conviction I would not live to see thirty still haunted me every day.

When I came out to Bruni, she shut off all contact with me, which was another huge blow. Bruni had always been my emotional rock. When we reconciled a year later, she told me that, with the AIDS epidemic in full swing, it wasn't my sexuality that bothered her, but the thought of having yet another person she loved snatched away. She just couldn't bear to watch someone else close to her die. I said, "I can't promise that's not going to happen, but I can promise to make smart choices." Fear of loss is not enough reason to sacrifice a relationship with the people who are still here.

Once the moment passed, she was all German efficiency. "Okay. Tell me about it. I want to learn," she stated.

I was taken aback, not quite sure how to explain it. "Well," I said, "you know how you loved Helmut?"

She nodded.

"Could you ever love another woman in that way?"

She was thoughtful for a moment and then said, "Perhaps."

"Well, I can't," I said. "I can only love men in that way. Not women at all."

"Oh," she said. "I see." And that was that. She was back to being the same old Bruni again and we were closer than ever.

After helping Judy with the divorce as best I could, I moved back down to Santa Barbara for the second time. I was a lost soul and ripe for the picking when I met Michael. He told me he had just gotten out of prison for embezzlement, but it was all behind him now. Being young, naive, and starved for love, I thought little of it and figured he paid his debt to society and deserved a second chance.

He swept me off my feet and proposed marriage after a short month of dating. This was long before it was legal. He bought me a beautiful golden retriever puppy for Christmas, whom I named Hope. I had loved animals ever since I was able to replace my old stuffed companions with real ones, and I fell for her on sight. He then convinced me to open a joint bank account.

Of the many things I learned from Judy, healthy money management was not one of them. It wasn't long before I got a call from the bank.

"There have been one or more deposits into your account that have raised flags in our system. Can you please come in as soon as possible?" The woman on the phone sounded official, but urgent.

It had to be some kind of mistake. I went down to the bank and sat across from a man with thick glasses who stared at my account on the screen.

"It looks like the person who opened the account with you has two social security numbers listed. That's why we called you in. We consider that something to be concerned about in finance. You might want to take a look at these."

He slid some papers across the desk. They were photocopies of checks Michael had deposited. My heart sank. Of course, he was embezzling from his employer again.

I called his company and was put in touch with the CFO, who thanked me for coming forward. He told me they had suspected Michael was stealing from the company, but they were having a hard time tracking it. I went down to the office and presented the copies the bank had given me.

That night, I couldn't sleep. I was still a people pleaser and loved Michael. I couldn't bear the thought of abandoning him in his time of need, but I couldn't abet his crimes either. When he inevitably lost his job, I called Judy and asked her if the two of us could move home until we figured out next steps. Being Judy, she agreed.

It didn't go well. Michael's charm and Judy's post-divorce vulnerability and carefree attitude toward spending were a terrible mix. I had brought a fox into the henhouse. Luckily, I could tell he was manipulating her before too much damage had been done. I kicked him out.

Not long after, I was pulled over as I was driving to the store. The officer came up to my window.

"Sir, would you mind stepping out of the vehicle, please?"

"What? Why? I wasn't even speeding."

"Yes, sir. There's a warrant out for your arrest. I'm going to need you to keep your hands where I can see them. Step out of the vehicle, please."

I was mortified.

My phone call was to Judy, who started working on my behalf as soon as she hung up the phone. She contacted a lawyer, started gathering information, and even put up her house for a loan to bail me out of jail.

It turned out that in addition to embezzling from his job and dropping the money into our joint account, Michael had also written over ten thousand dollars in bad checks while signing my name. Over the next few years, I was able to pay it all back with my mom's help, but it was an enormous sum at the time.

I never went to prison. Michael, however, ended up in the slammer multiple times. Criminals are never as smart as they think they are. The whole ordeal was also a huge relief for me in a way. It was the first time something terrible had happened and I wasn't blamed. Judy, despite her own recent heartbreak, stood by me without question and we figured it out together.

Around age twenty-four or twenty-five, I moved back from Santa Barbara for the final time. I went to business school and got an associate degree, which led to a better class of job. During this time, Judy made car payments, provided grocery money, rent, and constantly bailed me out. I was still trying to hold it all together, but my anxiety and depression were getting worse.

Although Judy gave me as much emotional and financial support as she could, I was still battling many of my demons alone. At last, I had a mom and a community, but I needed a family.

Despite my reunion with Jackie, I had had almost no contact with the rest of my biological family. Jackie was constantly disparaging other members of her family for not supporting her when she had me. She discouraged me from meeting them, and once I came out as gay, she made sure to let me know they were devoutly religious ("Holy Rollers," in her words) who would never accept me for who I was.

Naturally, when I received a surprise invitation to a family reunion in the Northern California town of Willits, I was jittery about meeting them all at once. I debated not going until the very last moment, but once there, I knew this was just what I had been searching for.

Among the other members of Jackie's family, I met her cousin, Shirley, a fashionable force of nature who took everything in stride. Shirley's husband, Terry, was kind but firm with steel-gray hair and compassionate eyes. He was the epitome of the wise father figure. Their three daughters, Stacy, Jenna, and Amy, were close to my age. The girls all sported brilliant azure eyes and charming smiles. Stacy and Amy had dark hair like their mother's, while Jenna had strawberry blond curls. I hit it off with the three of them and we exchanged contact information. I never expected to hear from them again, but a short time later, I received an invitation to a great aunt's birthday party with an offer to stay with the family over the weekend.

Again, I battled my anxiety up to the last minute, but I ended up making the long drive to the Northern California town of Blue Lake to stay with them.

I peered over my steering wheel as my car meandered up the dusty country track to their house. I pulled up in front of a charming home with redwood siding and a welcoming feel nestled in the forest. I stood on the porch and tried to work up the courage to ring the bell when Stacy opened the door with her husband in tow and a beautiful baby in her arms. The baby's name was Dante, and I fell in love with him at first sight.

The weekend that followed was one of the most profound and transformative of my life. From that first moment I arrived on their doorstep, I felt a sense of kinship that can only come from blood relations. These were my people in the truest sense of the word. They were kind and compassionate, but also didn't let me get away with anything. When I was in their home, it felt like *home*.

Part of the birthday celebrations included a dinner at a local casino. I had been reticent to talk about my experiences growing up, but after a few glasses of wine, the girls got me to share some of my stories. Terry and Shirley were shocked and heartbroken.

"We would have taken you, you know," Shirley piped in. "We heard CPS was coming to take you, but by the time we knew about it, it was too late. You were gone."

It had been a closed adoption. Jackie had kept silent about her parenting troubles until the last minute. When the state took me, they had cut me off from my entire family for fear she would find out where I was going and interfere with the adoption process.

Shirley's eyes welled, and Terry took her hand.

"We would have raised you as our son," she said, and I knew it was true.

The thought that I could have had a loving family, *this* family, all along was more than I could handle. I wept as the girls held my hands.

"I'm sorry to bring the party down," I said.

"No," said Terry. "This party is about your great aunt, but this moment is about you."

That weekend I thought a lot about what family meant to me. I realized that family is about actions, not blood. Judy was my mom. Jackie was not. It was as simple as that. I met with Jackie not long after and told her I would never be calling her "mom" again. In my mind, Judy had *earned* the title. Jackie took it well, but I don't think she believed me. I never wavered from that decision. I still loved her deeply and always did what I could for her, but I never thought of her as my mom again.

Over the next several months, I began making the trip up to Humboldt more and more as I dealt with my escalating mental health issues. I was living in San Francisco at twenty-eight and had just lost my job when I had a total breakdown.

I was in a very dark place one night. Part of me still *knew* I would die on the streets, and losing my job was just the beginning of the end. I still didn't know how to function in the world. I felt worthless and alone. I opened a beer. Then another. I had consumed five or six, but the pain in my heart was still there. I needed something stronger. I had an old bottle of Vicodin somewhere. I found it and fumbled it open, struggling with the tamper-resistant lid. The more I drank, the more pills I would take. With each dose, I felt the deep pit inside me slowly begin to close over. It was the first time in my life I could let go of past and future. It felt amazing, so I kept on going. Luckily, some instinct of self-preservation must have kicked in. I called Erica, who had since moved back to the area, and she called the paramedics.

I was admitted to the psychiatric ward of the hospital as a code 5150 (the code for self-harm) in the middle of the night and had to have a watch posted over me while I came down from the drugs and alcohol. But there's only so much a hospital can do. After a seventy-two-hour hold, I was released.

I came home to my empty apartment, no job, and only my dog, Hope, to greet me. Once again, the future stretched out before me like a void. I fell into the deepest despair of my life.

I wouldn't turn to Judy for help. She was dealing with her own problems, and I couldn't face burdening her with mine. I was no longer a child. I called

Terry and Shirley and asked if I could come up for a while to clear my head. They said, "Yes. Come up as soon as you can."

Erica drove me halfway. They met us in Laytonville and ferried me back up to Humboldt. I stayed in my room and slept for days. They gave me the space I needed but were always there with nonjudgmental emotional support and encouragement. They were smart enough to know I didn't need help or a bailout. I just needed someone to be there, to give me the room to help myself. I had to decide not to give up on my own.

When each of their daughters had been born, Terry had a tradition of buying his wife a small piece of jewelry to commemorate the occasion and serve as a reminder of the bond they had with each of their children. I learned later that when they had come to pick me up, Terry had gone out to a local flea market and gotten her a ring. He gave it to her with the words "This is for our boy." They were mine and I was theirs. They saw me at my most vulnerable, held out their arms, and caught me. It was the final piece of the puzzle. The only question that remained was what I was going to do next.

I made the decision to live.

I stayed in Humboldt for several weeks before I was able to return home. My first day back, I signed myself into a program for depression and anxiety and went to every single meeting. It was a six-week outpatient program at the world-renowned Langley Porter Psychiatric Institute at UCSF. This program gave me valuable tools to help me cope with my major depression and anxiety.

Not long after coming back from Humboldt, I was living in San Francisco when I got a parking ticket (a very common and expensive occurrence in the city). I was talking to Judy on the phone about it.

"I don't know what I'm going to do," I said. "I can't make this month's rent as it is."

"Don't worry, honey. Just send it to me and I'll take care of it."

"No," I said. "Thank you, but no. I'll make it work, somehow."

"Are you sure?"

"Yes. Thank you, but it's time I stood on my own two feet. If I can't handle a parking ticket, how do I handle everything else?"

In the end, I figured it out. It was a small thing, but it made me feel as though I might be able to step into the world as an adult—that I was more than just a burden. With my family around me, I was taking my first wobbly steps on my own.

A year later, I moved up to Humboldt. Terry, Shirley, and the girls gave me love and support, but also called me out and held me accountable for my actions. The year I spent up there gave me something even Juju could not—a sense of independence.

At age thirty, which I hadn't thought I would live to see, I decided I was done with pills. I dropped my depression and anxiety meds and used the techniques I had learned in the Langley Porter program to white-knuckle it through. In hindsight, this wasn't the smartest thing to do. I do not recommend stopping psychotropic medications cold turkey. The next few months were rough, but I stuck with it. I started working out and ended up losing more than a hundred pounds.

I got a job at UCSF working at the gym and worked my way up to a position assisting the dean of the School of Medicine, which was the most prestigious job I'd had. In 2004, I met a man named Chris and we got married.

CHAPTER 20

Parenting Challenges & Rewards (Part 1)

It wasn't long before Chris and I discussed adopting a child of our own. We attended a seminar aimed at scaring away unqualified prospective adoptive parents, but I wasn't fazed. I had seen and lived through worse.

Chris was shocked, however. "I had no idea what was going on in the system," he said. "But now, understanding what you went through and seeing how Juju changed your life makes me want to adopt more."

We asked the agency for a toddler and told them we preferred a boy.

One day while I was at work, my email pinged. They didn't have a toddler, they said, but they had an exceptional teenage girl. She had grown up in a difficult situation and had then lost both her parents to alcohol-related issues. She had lived with her grandparents in Southern California for less than six months before they sent her back to the San Francisco Bay Area with nothing but a little money. CPS picked her up as she was trying to register for school and placed her in foster care. Along with the email was a picture of a strikingly beautiful, sad-looking young woman.

I sat at my desk at work with tears in my eyes. There was something about the fact that this poor, sweet, young girl had been through so much but still had the determination to try to register herself for school that spoke to me. She was fifteen and her name was Antigone.

When I told Chris, he laughed at me as if I were insane. What would two thirty-five-year-old men know about a fifteen-year-old girl? Maybe it was the look on my face or maybe he just realized I was once one of those kids, but it didn't take long before he relented.

"I don't think it would hurt to invite her social worker over to talk about it," he said with a sigh.

We invited the social worker over the following Saturday and talked for over two hours. It was clear even then that the social worker was very attached to Antigone. We wondered why she didn't adopt the girl herself but didn't think much else about it at the time. It wasn't until later that we realized what a problem this would become. After the meeting, we went out for a walk.

"I know how it feels," I said to Chris, "to go through all the visitations and get your hopes up, only to have it snatched away. I don't think I could live with myself if we did that to her."

"So no trial period?" he asked.

"No trial period. If she comes, she's ours. She can call it off if she isn't interested, but she's already been rejected by one couple. Once we meet her, we're in."

Chris took my hand. "Okay."

"Okay?"

"Let's do this."

A few days later, we met her at a Chevy's in Berkeley. Over chips and salsa, we told her, in so many words, that we were all in. She looked surprised but was ready to come for a visit.

It started with a few weekends, but it wasn't long before we were working on the adoption paperwork. It took six months to finalize before she was our daughter in the eyes of the state. She had just turned sixteen at the time.

Chris and I knew adopting a teen would be a challenge, but we were as prepared as we could have been. We both tried to give Antigone a sense of belonging. I used all the tricks I had learned from Juju to make her feel loved and supported and like she always had a place to call home. We even drove several hours down to Bakersfield to pick up her dog, an old yellow lab, and brought him home.

When she came to us, she had been thinking of dropping out of school, but I told her that was not an option. Thinking back on my own youth, I knew the benefits of school went far beyond the scholastic. It was where she would make lasting friendships, develop social skills, and learn valuable life lessons. I told her, "We expect you to go to school and do your best."

She was a great kid. Because of her family history with alcohol, she didn't drink, do drugs, or run around with boys. I don't think she ever even missed curfew. She was eloquent for her age, intelligent, and beautiful. (I used to joke that I would go broke keeping up with her hair products.)

Unfortunately, the trauma of her early life appeared in ways even I was unprepared for. She was walled off, mistrustful, and as obstinate as her name-sake. It was difficult to bond with her. Everything had to be on her terms, and this is where I made mistakes.

As often happens to foster parents, especially those who were in the system themselves, her trauma triggered mine. I knew time was precious. We had a couple short years to prepare her for adult life. I was relentless in driving her to excel and succeed and demanded absolute respect, which, as I should have known from my time with the Roberts, was the wrong approach. Even Bruni chided me, saying, "She needs a friend more than a father," as she saw me pushing lessons from my past onto Antigone.

She had a couple of boyfriends. One of them was clearly in love with her despite the fact that the two of them were always fighting over something. He wanted to buy her a ring on one occasion. I absolutely refused. I still don't know why. It wasn't an engagement ring. Just an expression of caring for her, but something inside of me rebelled at the thought. It became another mean-ingless point of contention between us. Looking back, I wish I had relented.

Despite the conflicts they caused, my high expectations did help her succeed. Her grades skyrocketed just as mine had done. She made up all she had missed in school and got herself back on track. Chris and I told her it might be easier for her to do a fifth year of high school because catching up would be difficult, but she wasn't having it. Instead, she rose to the occasion, catching up while taking honors and advanced courses and graduating as a straight-A student.

She found relief from my nagging and rigid expectations with her social worker, who bought her all kinds of presents and often let her stay over. Once an adoption goes through, the social worker is supposed to be out of the picture, not act as a supplemental parent. There is a fine line between supporting the child and undermining the parents. I feel like this relationship further inflamed Antigone's resentment toward me.

My relationship with Chris was also crumbling, which didn't help matters. For reasons completely unrelated to the adoption, the love had gone out of our marriage. We stayed together for her sake another few years. By that time, she was old enough to be on her own, and the tension that had always existed between us blew up into open hostility.

She had always complied with my wishes, but became ever more bitter and insulting toward me, to the point of complete contempt. I even remember a few moments when she apologized to me and said that she had treated me unfairly, but it never lasted long. As defiant as I had been with Bruni in action, Antigone was with me in attitude.

At last, things came to a head. She was nineteen or twenty and going to junior college while living at home. Her disrespect was tearing our house apart. She announced she would be moving out.

"Fine," I said, "but I hope you don't expect me to keep making payments on the car we bought if you're taking it with you."

"Fine!" She stormed out of the room.

A few days later, she showed up with a new car.

"Where did you get the car?" I asked. "Is it insured?"

"It's none of your business," she shouted. I envisioned her getting pulled over or in a wreck without insurance. It was the last straw.

"That's it. I can't have you living here if you're going to treat me like this. You've got to go."

"Don't worry," she said, "I'm gone."

Even Chris, who had been able to form more of a bond with her, supported my decision. She, of course, went to live with her social worker. She wrote me a letter a year later saying, "I don't want to have any further contact with you." She hasn't spoken to me or my family since. I sent her a card on her thirtieth birthday. I never got a response.

I still love her and think of her as my daughter. That's never going to change. I often said to her, "Someday, you may prove you were right, and I'll apologize. Right now, you are just going to have to trust I'm making this decision because I love you and truly believe it's best for you." Now that I have more life experience, I do feel I owe her an apology. Maybe one day she'll be open to hearing it.

Parenting a foster child is a perilous and thankless job. You not only have to worry about what demons they bring to the relationship, but the demons you bring as well. On the whole, I am glad we did it. She went to college, and I believe she's married now because her last name has changed. She is an intelligent young woman and wasn't in the system for very long. She probably would have succeeded on her own in time, but the structure and love Chris and I gave her provided her with more tools to get there.

CHAPTER 21

Parenting Challenges & Rewards (Part 2)

I met Tony in the parking lot of a Home Depot while still married to Chris—if only on paper for Antigone's sake. Tony was married at the time as well. The affair was not something I'm proud of. Nor would one think it would lead to lasting love, but sometimes life smacks you when you least expect it, and your course is changed forever.

I had grown enough that with the grace and kindness of Tony's wife and a lot of communication and introspection, we were able to make it work without burning bridges or damaging lives. Tony's kids became my kids as well as his and his wife's, and somehow it all worked out in the end.

Tony became my rock—solid, strong, and gentle. We were married on my forty-third birthday—July 1, 2013, just a week after the Supreme Court had legalized same-sex marriage in all fifty states.

Two years prior, Tony's son, Nathan, had also gotten married. He was only nineteen or twenty at the time, and so was the girl. They had only been dating a few months. The entire family tried to talk him out of it. His new wife was one of five siblings born to a very young mother. Their family was struggling to make ends meet. About a year after they were married, they all moved into a small cottage next door to our property. Tony and I wanted to help them, but we were just starting out together as well.

One of Nathan's new in-laws was Domenic, a sweet, quiet boy of nine whom we had met when Nathan started dating his sister. As Domenic got older, we offered him odd jobs around our property to earn some cash and get away from the chaos at home. He was a kind, energetic boy with a somewhat feminine energy that made me wonder if he might be gay as well, at least when I met him. Once he hit puberty, there was no doubt he was straight.

When Nathan's in-laws moved out of the house next door and into a tiny travel trailer, we lost track of Domenic until he was just entering his sophomore year of high school. I reached out to offer him a temporary job helping us move into our new home. We were unloading boxes as we talked.

"So, how's school?"

"Um, yeah. It's okay, I guess," he said. "I might not be there much longer."

"Oh. I thought you would be a junior next year?"

"I think I might drop out." He shrugged as if this was no big deal.

"Can I ask why?"

He shrugged again and avoided eye contact. "Sophia's pregnant."

His little sister was just thirteen years old. Channeling my inner Juju, I gently pressed for more details. The family was still on the brink of poverty. When Sophia had gotten pregnant, Dom had been pushed to the side, and what little resources they had were devoted to her.

"Now, I take two buses to school every day. It takes me an hour and a half." On top of this, he had been diagnosed with a learning disability and ADHD, which his mother allowed him to use as an excuse not to work hard. It turned out he was failing every class. When Tony came home, I told him about Dom's situation.

"He's circling the drain," I said. "He's a good kid who's doing everything he can, but I don't think he'll make it without our help. He needs a mentor and an advocate at the school to get accommodations for his disabilities. Plus, he mostly just needs a ride."

"Okay," Tony agreed, but his tone was firm. "But I don't want him living here. And his mom has to agree."

The next day, I talked to Domenic and told him I believed we could help him, but he needed to be committed to doing the work. There could be no excuses if he wanted to graduate with his class. I also got his mother's permission, and we were off to the races.

We got him a car as Juju had done for me. I worked with the school to get him the help he needed. We enrolled him in sports, as I had been involved in track all those years ago. He was a natural athlete and had played football growing up, but his family's financial limitations never allowed him to do much more.

I picked him up and drove him to our house every day after school. I fed him and sat him down at the kitchen counter to do his homework. It wasn't long before his grades started improving. In a single semester, As and Bs replaced all the poor grades on his report card.

One afternoon during his first week with us, he came home smelling terrible. I realized he was wearing the same outfit as the day before. When I asked him about it, he looked embarrassed.

"I don't have any other clothes."

I shot Tony a look and he nodded in approval. I had Dom take a shower and put on some of Tony's old clothes for the next day, then I took him shopping. We didn't get anything fancy. Just essentials from a bargain department store, but I shoved him in a dressing room while I darted around trying to find anything I could that would fit him. *God,* I thought, catching my breath, *I really am turning into my mother!*

A few weeks later, Dom asked if he could come live with us. Life in the tiny trailer was becoming unbearable.

"You'll need to ask Tony," I said, fully expecting Tony to refuse.

When Dom sat across from him on the couch, however, Tony surprised me by relenting in an instant. I was so delighted, I cried. I asked his mother if she would allow us to become his legal guardians, and not long after, he came to stay.

Of course, the arrangement wasn't without its challenges. Once, when Tony and I were traveling, Dom was given permission to invite a "few" friends over, and it escalated out of control into a raging party. He was sure we would abandon him after that, just as I had been sure Juju would abandon me many times in my youth. Instead, when we got home, I just said, "You're tired. We're tired. You fucked up, but you're still our son. Go to bed."

The next day I "invited" all his party friends back under threat of extending the invitation to their mothers if they didn't show up. Tony sat them all down at the kitchen counter and had a very serious talk with the whole crew about consequences. The party was bad enough, but the fact that they all left Domenic to deal with the fallout when it got out of control was unacceptable.

"Domenic would go to bat and stand up for every one of you!" I said. "We expect you will do the same for him. Never abandon your friends if you want to be welcomed back into our home!"

Four wide-eyed, silent kids looked back at me in shock. Then Tony turned to them, and in his fiercest dad voice said, "And it better not fucking happen again!" All of the boys straightened their spines and nodded in agreement. Tony can be very intimidating when he wants to be.

The remainder of high school was a roller coaster for Domenic, just as my final year had been, but I have to give him credit. We pushed him hard, and he pushed back, but he did it. We provided him with every opportunity to make his dreams come true, but also allowed him the freedom to enjoy the final days of childhood (a lesson I learned from my mistake of pressuring Antigone).

When he graduated, he gave a speech almost thirty years to the day after I had given a speech at my own graduation thanking Juju for turning my life around. It was a touching moment that I'm glad Juju was there to see.

He ended his speech with:

You can't make it alone. Find others with the same ideas, same goals, same dreams, and value those who are around you. Those who see the best in you, those who want you to succeed and push you to do better than you thought. Be there for those who need someone because when you need someone, they'll be there for you.

Through my tears, I looked at Juju and said, "This is your legacy. You did this!" She was crying too. She loved Domenic as her grandson from the very beginning, and I could see the pride she had in him as he walked across the stage and accepted his diploma.

CHAPTER 22

Lessons Learned

Tony and I have helped raise several beautiful children and stepchildren. I've helped others wherever I can. I have spoken to foster care organizations on behalf of those who can't speak for themselves. I've tried to prepare would-be foster parents for the realities they will face should they take on the incredible burden and privilege of being a troubled child's only lifeline to a sense of self-worth.

In some ways the foster system has improved dramatically since the '70s and '80s. Now, placement with blood relatives is a priority, screening for prospective foster and adoptive parents is much more stringent, and sensitivity with regards to race, sexuality, and gender is given much more weight and training.

Many of the problems I encountered, however, are much the same. The system is pathetically underfunded. It seems whenever funding is cut, it is first removed from social services. Social workers, judges, and psychologists still struggle with enormous caseloads and few resources. Foster parents are often overloaded as well.

Love is not always enough. Those who take on the responsibility of foster parenting or adopting need to be prepared for a difficult and thankless job. It is a job requiring bravery, incredible communication and listening skills, understanding, and patience. You have to be able to face your own trauma, but also to let it go and realize the needs of your child are not the same as yours were. You have to provide structure and healthy boundaries, but also a sense of peace, forgiveness, and above all, stability.

You have so much power over the life of another—more than you may ever know. The best things you can learn to say as a foster parent are "just hang on," "it's not your fault," "tell me how I can help," "you're going to be just fine," and, of course, "I'm here, and I'm not going anywhere."

Recognizing that not everyone has the time, resources, or personality to foster a child, there are other ways to be involved. It's not hard to create magic for a child. You can volunteer, mentor, donate, start a toy drive, or work as an advocate. There are also important roles that don't require as much time and energy as foster parenting. Being a "Big Brother" or "Big Sister," or a CASA (Court Appointed Special Advocate), GAL (Guardian Ad Litem), or just a constant figure in the life of a child can be a lifesaving act. I think about how many relationships in my story end with "I never saw them again." Anything that minimizes the damaging sense of impermanence is of immeasurable value.

In fact, you've already done something just in purchasing this book. A portion of the proceeds will go directly to benefit foster children in Juju's name through the Valley of the Moon Children's Foundation. If you'd like to make an additional donation or learn more about the program, please see the final page of this book or visit my website at www.ginomedeiros.com.

If there are any kids in foster care who are reading this, know that you are not alone and that it will get better. Reach out if you can. Don't be silent. Advocate for yourself or find someone who will advocate for you. Take advantage of all the benefits and training the system has to offer so you're as prepared for the adult world as you possibly can be. It might seem cold, unfeeling, and institutional at times, but it exists to help you, and you can find gems in the mud if you look hard enough.

Finally, to those who may read this book, put it down, and decide direct action is not for them, know that you can still make a difference. Ultimately, this is a problem with our society. How we live as a community can be measured in how we treat the most disadvantaged among us, particularly our children. Community is crucial, as the community of Livermore was to me. If you teach your own kids to be accepting of others, make sure to include disadvantaged kids in birthday parties and events, speak to your friends and other parents in the community, and most of all, remember them when you vote—you may be doing more than you know. The problems with the system today exist because it is taboo to talk about it. Silence allows it to fester. Have a voice and you will allow others to find theirs.

I look forward to a day with no more broken boys and girls.

Epilogue

In late May of 2022, I took Juju to the ER, where they discovered the ovarian cancer she had fought so fiercely against had returned with a vengeance. It was everywhere. In a way, her decline enabled me to pick up this book and start working on it again after not being able to face it for years.

As much as it is my story, it is also the story of the power of kindness and how much a single person can change the path of a life. Juju gave me a gift that I am now dedicated to paying forward. My continued support of the children in the foster care system and this book are a part of that, as well as my relationship with my stepchildren, whom I now see as my own.

I remember one time close to the end of her life when Juju was very confused. I was lying in the bed next to hers and holding her hand. She was having trouble remembering where she was and why she was there. I asked her, "Do you know who I am?" and she responded with, "I'm dying, honey, I'm not stupid! You're my son, my joy." Then she fell asleep.

In the end, I was able to give back to her as well. Tony and I, with help from Mary, were able to grant Juju some peace and financial stability until she passed away on July 15, 2022. There is a hole in my heart that will never go away. It's never easy to lose a parent, but the loss of someone like Juju, who gave her love more freely than many biological parents do and who saved my life through sheer force of kindness, was especially hard.

I often think back on another rare moment of lucidity toward the end when she looked up at me as I was preparing to go home and said, "Thank you for always showing up for me!"

"I will always show up for you, Juju!" I said. "And do you know why?"

"Because I always showed up for you."

"You're damn right!" I said.

I am proud Tony and I were able to step up for her at the end of her life. Caring for her was filled with its own struggles and challenges, but I think we succeeded in filling her final years with as much joy, happiness, and appreciation as possible.

Her legacy of kindness lives on.

Becky is another story. She never really accepted me or Mary into the family and had sided with Juju's husband, Frank, in their divorce. Since then, she's had her own struggles with money, among other problems. I realized (luckily in time) that she was benefiting from our mother's decline through how she "managed" Juju's finances. The amount of money she took from our mom is staggering. She insisted on labeling herself as an "only child," even to the doctors and nurses in hospice.

This was part of the reason for the adoption. Found family is important, but without legal recognition, it can fall apart in difficult times. If Juju hadn't adopted me, Becky would have taken over everything and I would have had no legal recourse. Juju made the choice to empower me and, by extension, Mary. She loved Becky, but Becky had lost her trust. Juju knew Mary and I would be shut out of her end-of-life care and even her memorial if Becky had the legal last word. Mary was never officially adopted. She didn't want to be. But Juju made me promise never to cast her aside or leave her out of the loop. I've kept that promise.

In 1994, I got a frantic call from Claudia. The police had found Anne dead in her Florida home. The Casey Family Program paid for me to fly out to Florida, where I was reunited with Claudia and Maria. When we got to the house, it was like a nightmare had come to life. Anne's mental health had deteriorated over the years. The house was beyond filthy and crammed with so much hoarded debris that we could barely enter it. Anne had been living there with seven dogs. Every single surface was covered in garbage and ruined stuff. The toilets and sinks were all caked in a black coating, and the bed had been chewed on by the dogs. There was one tiny oval of visible floor in the bedroom where they had found Anne's body.

You would have thought Anne was poverty-stricken based on her surroundings, but her mother had died not too many years earlier and had left her a significant sum. Anne owned her house outright. She had left no will, and since, by law, Claudia and Maria were her only adopted children, they stood to inherit over a million dollars and the house. They asked me to help them clean it up and set Anne's affairs in order and promised to make sure I got a share of the inheritance as well. Once the house was clean, however, they disappeared and I never saw a penny.

While going through Anne's mail as part of the housecleaning, I came across a card from Bruni, who had remained friends with Anne until the end and even flew out to see her a couple of times. True to Bruni's nature, thinking Anne was poor, she had tucked a $100 bill inside.

Maria had always struggled with health issues and died in 2010 of COPD. Claudia divorced her husband and now lives in London. We're no longer in touch.

Although Antigone is no longer in contact with me, I will always be there for her. My support is not conditional upon her being there for me, just as Juju's was never conditional on my being there for her. When I signed on the dotted line and made her my daughter, I knew it was a lifelong commitment.

I will keep reaching out to her and apologizing for the mistakes I made, but I also feel Chris and I helped her overall and contributed to her success, and for that I am proud.

On May 14, 2012, Jackie passed away in my arms while Tony held me and Erica held her hand. She was 62. She had fought lung cancer for more than 10 years. Despite the tumultuous relationship we shared for most of my life, her death devastated me. It took time to adjust to her loss, but she was able to give me something towards the end of her life that I am eternally grateful for: an apology and full ownership over what had happened. She held my face as she told me that she needed to know that I would be ok after she was gone. After 42 years, my mother showed up and mothered me. It was a powerful moment that ultimately brought me a sense of peace I had never dared hope for.

Bruni and I remained close. She was a force of nature, insisting on driving up to see Tony and me often and continuing to make cakes every year for my birthday. In 2018, I came over to help her with the cake, but found it already sitting on the counter with her nowhere in sight. I knew right away something was wrong. I was so worried about where she was that I ran through the house calling out for her. Running down the back hall, I heard the faint sound of her voice from what used to be my room. When I went through the bedroom door, I found her lying on her back on the bed and knew she was very ill. She had been hiding it well and insisted on going about her day once I had helped her up as if nothing had happened, but I knew.

That day she casually asked me about California's recently passed law allowing for people with terminal illnesses to pass away with medical assistance. When she said it out loud, it cut through me like a knife. I wanted to beg her not to do it, but I also knew that when she made up her mind she would never be swayed.

I took her hand, looked her in the face and said, "Bruni, that is not what I want for you, but I also know there is nothing I can say to change your mind. This is your journey, and I will do whatever you need to support you."

She started giving me things. One day, she gave me a stack of photo albums, a record of her life with me, but also before me. Among the albums were photos from the war of lost friends and relatives with Nazi regalia in the background. There was also Freddy's baby book and several books of images from my childhood. There were smiling photos of Helmut. The books contained all the painful and emotional memories from Bruni's life of loss.

When Bruni died, I was the first person they called. I returned the albums to her house but asked that Freddy's baby book be cremated with her.

Bruni always loved a treasure hunt. When I was younger, whenever she sent anything in the mail, she always hid a hundred-dollar bill somewhere. When my kids were growing up, she often sent them the most hideous jacket or sweater, and they would give me a look of extreme disappointment. I just smiled and told them not to get rid of it until they had searched everywhere. Sure enough, there was always at least a hundred dollars hidden somewhere.

That last birthday, along with the cake, she had given me a couple of coffee cans of old coins. Because of all the emotion surrounding her death, I didn't bother to go through them until years later. When I did, I found valuable family heirlooms that consisted of several pieces of diamond jewelry, many over a hundred years old. Tony had several of the stones reset into a wedding set for me. I then surprised him with a solid platinum ring with Bruni's diamonds all the way around it. In the forty years I had known her, I had never seen the jewelry. She never wore them. That's not the type of person she was.

I saw C.C. again during my senior year of high school. I was able to get back in touch with Kathy from the Children's Garden and arrange a visit. They lived in New Jersey, so of course Juju bought me a ticket. I flew out for a few days to meet with them and reconnect with C.C., but things had changed.

C.C. was struggling. He was no longer the bright-eyed, mischievous kid I had known all those years ago. I felt like we were two soldiers who had been through a war and come out the other side, only to find the trauma was all we had in common. It was an awkward reunion at best.

Time, however, has incredible healing powers. In writing this book, I reached out to him again. He responded, and we spoke for hours. It was as if no time had passed between us. We are now so in sync and effortlessly connected, it's like having my brother back again.

Through our reconnection, I learned his life with Kathy and Leo had its own difficulties. Adoption was not the ticket to happiness I had always imagined it would be for him. It was Leo who had really wanted to adopt him. C.C. always felt like Kathy favored me. When the couple divorced and Kathy found a new partner, C.C. felt even more like a consolation prize. Eventually, he resorted to the defense mechanism he knew best. He ran. Kathy didn't come after him, and they haven't spoken in years.

She's been in contact with me, though, and now that C.C. and I have found each other, perhaps there is another chapter or two left in their story.

Domenic attended Humboldt State on nearly a full-ride scholarship. I did everything possible to get as much paid for as we could. Tony and I had saved all the money the state sent us for taking him in with the hope of using it to offset some of his college expenses, just as Frank had done for me so many years ago. Then COVID hit. Domenic struggled and lost his way a bit. The pandemic pushed him off track and he started making decisions Tony and I could not support. He got involved with some shady people while in Humboldt and did not want to go back to school. His poor choices continued when he moved home. In the end, Tony and I had to ask him to move out of our house. I was heartbroken and I cried every day for a week.

He was only twenty years old, and I worried he was not prepared for life as an adult, but I also knew I could not allow his poor choices to affect the rest of our family. He dropped out of touch soon after he left and went down a dark path, no doubt thinking, as I had done, that he never deserved our love and we had finally abandoned him. I made it clear, however, that just because we couldn't have him in our house didn't mean we were turning our backs. He's still my son, and that's never going to change. Juju taught me once you bring a child into your life and make them yours, you never walk away from them, and I never will.

Recently, Dom has been emailing more often. He says he's going back to school. I have high hopes for him, but whatever happens, family is family. Juju's legacy of unwavering belief in those she loved, even when they didn't believe in themselves, is still upheld and continues through me, my kids, Tony, and Mary.

As I write this, I am in the kitchen of the house Tony and I have built. We run a successful business and own property just a short drive from where the old Dependent Unit was. Life goes on, with all the drama, tempers, pettiness, and problems that come with a family, but surrounded with love and belonging too. In every corner and hidden away in boxes are the memories of a childhood that shouldn't have been allowed to happen: Bruni's stained-glass window, the album from Children's Garden, the quilts from the Dependent Unit, the awkward letter from my birth father. Each is a piece to a puzzle and a reminder that it's never too late to change your course or someone else's for the better.

Life is good.

ACKNOWLEDGEMENTS

A huge thank you to my husband Tony for fifteen years of uncompromising support and compassion. This book was an emotional labor of love and I never would have finished it without your steady and compassionate influence. You are my rock.

Thanks also to my incredible editor, Kris Gucker, for his wordsmithing skill in filling in the gaps and polishing what started as a journal into the finished book you see today. I appreciate your tireless work and craft in keeping this manuscript on track and on message. This story wouldn't be what it is without your knowledge and guidance. You are a rare gem!

To my proofreader, Michael Burge, thank you for your amazing attention to detail and for fitting this project into your busy schedule.

To all of the current and former foster children out there: We are and always will be connected as brothers and sisters. Together, I know we can change the system so no one else has to suffer.

To my family and friends that have watched me on this journey, your love and support over the years has been instrumental in helping me get to where I am. I am especially grateful to my late Aunt Terry who had the courage to seek me out despite being told not to. Because of her efforts, I was able to reconnect with my biological family. She was instrumental in my current happiness

And a special thanks to the late Maya Angelou who encouraged me to write about my experiences. The seed she planted has grown, I hope it will encourage and inspire others to tell their stories as an act of healing. She would be proud.

HOW TO HELP

In 2023, in conjunction with The Valley of the Moon Children's Foundation, I launched *The Judy Welsh Foster Youth Transition Award*. This award serves as a tribute to Judy's enduring legacy and her compassionate spirit, especially towards young adults transitioning from the foster care system into adulthood. While there are countless programs geared towards scholars who are college bound, there is a gap for those who are simply trying to survive. The goal of this program is to help those young people as they fumble into adulthood with little to no help or guidance. I will also be donating a portion of the proceeds of this book to my mom's fund. If you are able, I ask that you consider donating as well.

To donate online, please visit Valley of the Moon Children's Foundation website at https://www.vomcf.org/donate-today.

Be sure to specify your donation is for "The Judy Welsh Foster Youth Transition Award" in the comments section.

To donate by check, please make checks payable to Valley of the Moon Children's Foundation and mention "Judy's Fund" in the memo section of your check.

Valley of the Moon Children's Foundation
The Judy Welsh Foster Youth Transition Award
PO Box 11671
Santa Rosa, CA 95406

Your tax-deductible contributions will help carry forward Judy's legacy, offering essential support to young adults who are transitioning from foster care into their new phase of life.